FOOD
FOR LOVE

FOOD
FOR LOVE

Hannah Baskerville

hamlyn

Published in the UK in 1998
by Hamlyn, a division of Octopus Publishing Group Ltd
2-4 Heron Quays, London E14 4JP

This edition published 2002 by Octopus Publishing Group Ltd

Copyright ©1998, 2002 Octopus Publishing Group Ltd

ISBN 0 600 60823 9

Printed in China

All rights reserved. No part of this publication may be
reproduced, stored in a retrieval system or transmitted in
any form or by any means, electronic, mechanical,
photocopying, recording or otherwise, without the written
permission of the publisher.

NOTES

Both metric and imperial measurements have been given in all
recipes. Use one set of measurements only and not a
mixture of both.

Standard level spoon measurements are used in all recipes.
1 tablespoon = one 15 ml spoon
1 teaspoon = one 5 ml spoon

Eggs should be medium to large unless otherwise stated.
The Department of Health advises that eggs should not be
consumed raw. This book contains dishes made with raw or lightly
cooked eggs. It is prudent for more vulnerable people such as
pregnant and nursing mothers, invalids, the elderly, babies and
young children to avoid uncooked or lightly cooked dishes made
with eggs. Once prepared, these dishes should be kept refrigerated
and used promptly.

Milk should be full fat unless otherwise stated.

Meat and poultry should be cooked thoroughly. To test if poultry
is cooked, pierce the flesh through the thickest part with a skewer
or fork – the juices should run clear, never pink or red. Do not re-
freeze poultry that has been frozen previously and thawed.
Do not re-freeze a dish that has been frozen previously.

Pepper should be freshly ground black pepper unless
otherwise stated.
Fresh herbs should be used, unless otherwise stated. If unavailable,
use dried herbs as an alternative but halve the quantities stated.

Measurements for canned food have been given as a standard
metric equivalent.

Nuts and nut derivatives
This book includes dishes made with nuts and nut derivatives. It is
advisable for customers with known allergic reactions to nuts and
nut derivatives and those who may be potentially vulnerable to
these allergies, such as pregnant and nursing mothers, invalids, the
elderly, babies and children, to avoid dishes made with nuts and
nut oils. It is also prudent to check the labels of pre-prepared
ingredients for the possible inclusion of nut derivatives.

Vegetarians should look for the 'V' symbol on a cheese to ensure it
is made with vegetarian rennet. There are vegetarian forms of
Parmesan, Feta, Cheddar, Cheshire, Red Leicester, dolcelatte and
many goats' cheeses, among others.
Ovens should be preheated to the specified temperature –
if using a fan-assisted oven, follow the manufacturer's
instructions for adjusting the time and the temperature.

All recipes serve two unless stated otherwise.

Contents

Introduction   6

Starters   10

Main Courses   24

Salads & Vegetables   40

Desserts   50

Cakes & Biscuits   68

Celebration Menus   82

Index   96

Introduction

Throughout history, lovers all over the world have relied on a variety of love potions enhanced with the magical charms of enchantment to soften hearts that remained stubbornly impervious to the advance of cupid's bow. This might mean a secret ingredient slipped into a goblet of wine, or an elaborate concoction of something rather more complicated. The rarer an ingredient was, the more likely it was thought to hold aphrodisiac qualities.

But anyone who has prepared a candlelit meal for a loved one knows only too well the potential power of food. Food has been associated with love since time immemorial. There's something gloriously intimate about two people who love each other sharing a meal together.

From an impromptu glass of fine wine to the most elaborate, lovingly prepared meal, the act of preparing food for someone speaks a lot louder – and more eloquently – than any spoken words can ever hope to do. It says 'I am looking after you, you are worth every effort I can make, I love you.'

Many a romance has been sealed over a cosy tête à tête meal and special romantic meals continue to punctuate a relationship over the years: a series of celebrations to mark an anniversary each year; birthday treats; and simple meals that just happen in an impromptu kind of way to say 'You're special.'

Just picture the scene: the two of you walking hand in hand across a moonlit beach until you come to your favourite little taverna, where you sit opposite each other, bathed in the warm glow of the candles, and eat a delicious meal with a bottle of wine, chilled to just the right temperature.

We can't lay on the moonlit beach, but the rest is well within your capabilities. The food, the wine, each other ... the rest is up to you!

THE FOOD

The food that you choose for the romantic occasion for two has to be right. This is no time for fish and chips or toad in the hole followed by steamed roly poly pudding or jelly and custard. Nice as all these foods can be, everything has its time and its place, and a candlelit meal for two is right for neither.

We've made a variety of suggestions throughout this book and we hope they strike the right chord with you. We've arranged our suggestions in the conventional way – starters, main courses, vegetables and salads, desserts and cakes.

Try Smoked Oyster Tarts followed by Roast Pheasant with Calvados and Red Fruit Salad. Or Wild Mushroom Feuilleté followed by Lobster Thermidor and Chocolate Bread and Butter Pudding.

To give you a helping hand, just in case you're short of inspiration, the book ends with three delicious three-course menus. We've suggested Artichoke and Hazelnut Soup, Duck with Blackcurrants and French Bean Bundles, and Chocolate Mousse to finish. Or you might prefer Liver Pâté, followed by Pork Noisettes with Chicory and Beetroot Salad, and Ratafia Ice Cream to finish. Or alternatively Ceviche of Salmon followed by Fillet Steak Piquant with Stuffed Tomatoes and Chocolate Mousse Tartlets to finish.

Whichever menu you choose, it will be absolutely delicious and we fervently hope these have the desired effect of capturing that special, intimate, romantic moment.

SETTING THE SCENE

The setting does not need to be lavish or extravagant, but it nevertheless deserves some careful thought. Low lighting, gentle background music, add these to the mouth-watering aromas that herald the delicious meal you've prepared with

love, and the atmosphere is set.

A simple touch will often do just as well as anything more elaborate. A single rose on the breakfast tray, for example, a candle on the dinner table, a beautifully laid table with a few hints of lace and a stylish little posy as its centrepiece, these are all simple but all-important gestures that say you've made

an effort because you're eating with someone special who means more to you than anything in the world.

THE LANGUAGE OF FLOWERS

Everybody likes to be given flowers. They speak lovingly and intimately when people can't. The deep red, velvety rose of love, the virgin white rose of purity, the unopened buds of innocence, the carefree wildness of violets, the formality of one exquisite orchid, there is an appropriate flower for every imaginable situation. Flowers run the gamut of the emotions.

Add them to your vocabulary and allow them to speak for you. You'll never regret it.

AN ESSENTIAL INGREDIENT

You'll notice, no doubt – and probably with glee – that chocolate plays an important part in this book. Many of the desserts and cakes given here owe their raison d'être to chocolate.

This is no accident. Chocolate is, for many people, a gloriously seductive ingredient, tempting, wicked and utterly irresistible. A rich chocolate dessert seems the perfect end to a romantic meal.

There is an increasingly wide range of different types of chocolate available. Careful selection of the right one will take you half way to culinary success.

Plain Chocolate

This is generally the best chocolate to use for cooking, although the quality can vary considerably. Choose a chocolate that contains a high proportion of 'cocoa solids'.

This can vary from anywhere between 30 and 70 per cent, and should be specified on the wrapping. Although chocolate containing a higher proportion of cocoa solids will be more expensive, it will give a much stronger and smoother flavour.

Milk Chocolate

This contains between 15 and 30 per cent cocoa solids and has plenty of additional cream and sugar. It has a less intense chocolate flavour but it is useful for contrasting decorations. Chopped chunks add a delicious creamy bite to cakes and biscuits.

White Chocolate

This gets its flavour from 'cocoa butter', which is extracted during the chocolate processing. It is high in fat and sugar and is more likely to burn when melting. Luxury brands of white chocolate will give a richer, less sugary flavouring.

Cocoa Powder

This is another product of chocolate processing and has a strong bitter flavour. It is useful in cakes and cookies and in some desserts and puddings to accentuate the flavour of the chocolate.

Drinking chocolate powder, which is used for making hot milk drinks, is not the same thing at all and is not a substitute for cocoa powder.

Melting Chocolate

Break plain, milk or white chocolate into even-sized pieces and put in a heatproof bowl. Place the bowl over a saucepan containing a little gently simmering water, and leave until melted. (Make sure that the base of the bowl is not in contact with the water or the chocolate will overheat; make sure, too, that the water does not boil away.)

Gently stir the chocolate and leave it over the water for a little longer if any lumps remain. Remove from the heat, making sure that droplets of water on the bowl do not come into contact with the chocolate. (This solidifies the texture of the chocolate, making it difficult to use for decorative purposes.)

Melting Chocolate in the Microwave

Break plain, milk or white chocolate into pieces and put in a bowl (not a metal one). The melting times will vary according to the amount of chocolate being melted, the type of bowl, and the temperature of the chocolate. As a rough guide, allow about 2 minutes on HIGH for 125 g/4 oz plain chocolate, and 2–3 minutes on MEDIUM for milk and white chocolate, which have a greater tendency to burn.

Let the chocolate stand for 2 minutes after microwaving, heating it for a little longer if there are still any lumps after standing.

Chocolate Decorations

These decorations make the perfect finishing touch for your special chocolate desserts and gâteaux. They can be made up to two weeks in advance and stored in an airtight container in a cool place.

If the chocolate is brittle and crumbles when you attempt

to make chocolate curls or shavings, it may be too cold. If this is so, leave it for a while at room temperature to soften slightly.

Chocolate Leaves

Clean your chosen leaves, such as bay, mint or rose. Melt 50 g/2 oz plain, milk or white chocolate (this will cover about 15 leaves). Using a paintbrush, thickly coat the undersides of the leaves, taking the chocolate almost to the edges of the leaves. Leave to set on a baking tray lined with greaseproof paper. Once the chocolate is set, carefully peel away the leaves from the chocolate.

Chocolate Curls

Spread the chocolate on to the surface. When just set, push a clean wallpaper scraper across the surface to make the curls. Mini-curls can be made by using a narrower scraper.

Quick Chocolate Curls

Allow a large bar of plain, milk or white chocolate to soften in a warm room. Use a vegetable peeler, or a sharp knife as

shown, to shave off curls. These can be added to cakes and puddings or even sprinkled on hot chocolate to add that finishing touch.

Starters

Potato Salad with Smoked Salmon, Grapes and Pecan Nuts

- 300 g/10 oz waxy potatoes, boiled and sliced
- 25 g/1 oz smoked salmon, cut into thin strips
- 125 g/4 oz cooked peeled prawns
- 50 g/2 oz seedless white grapes, halved
- 25 g/1 oz pecan nuts
- 1 tablespoon snipped fresh chives
- 1 tablespoon chopped fresh dill, to garnish

DRESSING:
- 1 tablespoon mayonnaise
- 2 tablespoons soured cream
- 1 teaspoon lemon juice
- salt and freshly ground black pepper

1 Put the sliced potatoes in a bowl and mix in the smoked salmon, prawns, grapes, nuts and chives.
2 Whisk together all the dressing ingredients
3 Pour the dressing over, toss lightly and sprinkle with dill.

Preparation time: 15 minutes
Cooking time: 15–20 minutes

Quails' Egg Tartlets

- 15 g/½ oz butter or margarine
- 2 sheets of filo pastry

FILLING:
- 3 quails' eggs
- 40 g/1½ oz cream cheese
- 1 tablespoon grated Parmesan cheese
- little cayenne pepper

TO GARNISH:
- sprigs of chervil
- salad leaves

1 Melt the butter or margarine and use a little to brush the baking tins.
2 Place the first sheet of filo pastry on the board (keep the rest covered so they do not dry out). Brush with a little melted butter or margarine, add the second sheet, fold in half and brush again, then add the third sheet and brush again.
3 Cut six rounds from the triple thickness and press into the tins. Bake in a preheated oven, 200°C/400°F/Gas Mark 6, for about 5 minutes. Allow to cool.
4 Put the eggs into boiling water and cook for 2 minutes. Cool and halve.
5 Meanwhile, blend the cream and Parmesan cheeses together, adding a shake of cayenne. Spoon or pipe into the pastry cases.
6 Top with the halved eggs. Sprinkle with more cayenne pepper. Garnish with chervil and a little salad.

Preparation time: 15 minutes
Cooking time: 5 minutes
Oven temperature: 200°C/400°F/Gas Mark 6

O, my Love is like a red, red rose
That's newly sprung in June:
O, my Love is like the melodie
That's sweetly play'd in tune.

ROBERT BURNS 1759–96

Wild Mushroom Feuilleté

- **225 g/8 oz frozen puff pastry, thawed**
- **5 g/¼ oz butter or margarine**
- **225 g/8 oz closed cup mushrooms, sliced**
- **175 g/6 oz oyster mushrooms, sliced**
- **150 ml/¼ pint soured cream**
- **150 ml/¼ pint single cream**
- **1 garlic clove, crushed**
- **salt and freshly ground black pepper**

1 Roll out the pastry to about 5 mm/¼ inch thick and cut out three 12 cm/5 inch circles and three 7 cm/3 inch ones. Place the circles on a baking tray, bake in a preheated oven, 230°C/450°F/Gas Mark 8, for 10–12 minutes, until puffed up and golden brown.

2 Meanwhile, melt the butter or margarine and fry the closed cup mushrooms for 3 minutes. Add the oyster mushrooms and cook for 2 minutes, until tender.

3 Remove the mushrooms with a slotted spoon and boil the remaining liquid rapidly until reduced to about ½ tablespoon. Add the mushrooms, soured and single creams, garlic and seasoning. Reheat gently without boiling.

4 To serve, place some mushroom mixture and liquid on top of each large pastry circle. Cover each with a smaller pastry circle and serve.

Preparation time: 20 minutes
Cooking time: 10–12 minutes
Oven temperature: 230°C/450°F/Gas Mark 8

Florence-Style Eggs

- **50 g/2 oz spinach**
- **2 eggs**
- **2 tablespoons double cream**
- **2 tablespoons grated Parmesan cheese**
- **25 g/1 oz butter, cut into pieces**
- **salt and freshly ground black pepper**

1 Wash the spinach and place in a pan with the water still clinging to it after washing. Heat over moderate heat for a few minutes until the spinach wilts. Drain and leave to cool.

2 When it has cooled a little, force as much water as you can through a colander by pushing with a wooden spoon. Divide the spinach in half and spoon into the bottom of two individual ovenproof ramekins or cocotte dishes.

3 Break an egg on top of each mound of spinach and top with a spoonful of double cream. Spoon over a tablespoon of grated Parmesan and add a few pieces of butter. Bake in a preheated oven, 190°C/350°F/Gas Mark 5, for 15 minutes.

Preparation time: 10 minutes
Cooking time: 15 minutes
Oven temperature: 190°C/350°F/Gas Mark 5

Warm Salad with Calves' Liver

- **1 large leaf feuille de chêne, frisée, escarole or lambs lettuce**
- **2 large leaves radicchio**
- **75 g/3 oz small mangetout, topped and tailed**
- **2 tablespoons olive oil**
- **125 g/4 oz calves' liver, cut into fine strips**
- **1 spring onion, sliced**
- **2 tablespoons lemon juice**
- **salt and freshly ground black pepper**
- **little chopped marjoram, to garnish**

1 Tear up the leaves and arrange them on 2 serving plates. Blanch the mangetout in boiling salted water for 3–4 minutes, then scatter them on top of the lettuce.
2 Heat the olive oil in a large pan. Fry the strips of liver and spring onions for about 2 minutes over a fairly high heat, turning them frequently until they are evenly coloured, but leaving the liver slightly pink in the middle.
3 Stir in the lemon juice and season to taste.

4 Spoon the liver mixture over the salad leaves and strew marjoram on top. Serve immediately.

Preparation time: 15 minutes
Cooking time: 5–6 minutes

Smoked Oyster Tarts

- **250 g/½ lb shortcrust pastry**
- **50 g/2 oz smoked oysters, drained and chopped**
- **1 teaspoon chopped fresh parsley**
- **1 egg**
- **150 ml/¼ pint single cream**
- **pinch of cayenne pepper**
- **freshly ground black pepper**

1 Roll out the dough thinly and cut into rounds using a 6 cm/2½ inch cutter. Line 12 greased mini tartlet tins with the dough rounds and prick all over with a fork.
2 Bake the pastry cases 'blind' in a preheated oven, 220°C/425°F/Gas Mark 7, for 10 minutes. Remove from the oven and reduce the heat to 190°C/375°F/Gas Mark 5.
3 Divide the oysters and parsley between the pastry cases.
4 Mix together the egg and cream and season to taste with cayenne and pepper. Pour the mixture into the pastry cases.
5 Bake the tarts for a further 15–20 minutes or until the filling is set and golden brown.

Makes about 12
Preparation time: 20 minutes
Cooking time: 30 minutes
Oven temperature: 220°C/425°F/Gas Mark 7, then 190°C/375°F/Gas Mark 5

Spicy Butterflied Prawns

- **500 g/1 lb prawns**
- **MARINADE:**
- **25 ml/1 fl oz orange juice**
- **2 tablespoons lime juice**
- **3 tablespoons olive oil**
- **1 teaspoon white rum**
- **1 garlic clove, crushed**
- **1 teaspoon dried green peppercorns, crushed**
- **1 small hot dried red chilli, crushed**
- **salt**

1 Remove the shells and tails from the prawns, then slit each one part way through down the back, so that they open up and lie flat. Rinse to remove the dark vein, then pat dry.
2 Combine all the marinade ingredients, with salt to taste, in a mixing bowl. Add the prawns to the marinade and stir. Cover and leave to marinate in the refrigerator for at least 4 hours.

3 Thread the prawns on to skewers, inserting the point of the skewer at the tail end and pushing it through the prawn to come out at the head end. Reserve the marinade.
4 Grill the prawns over hot coals for 6–10 minutes, turning and basting occasionally with the reserved marinade. Be careful not to overcook the prawns. They are cooked when they change from translucent to opaque. Serve hot.

Preparation time: 15 minutes, plus at least 4 hours marinating
Cooking time: 6–10 minutes

Love looks not with the eyes, but with the mind,
And therefore is wing'd Cupid painted blind.

WILLIAM SHAKESPEARE 1564–1616
A MIDSUMMER NIGHT'S DREAM

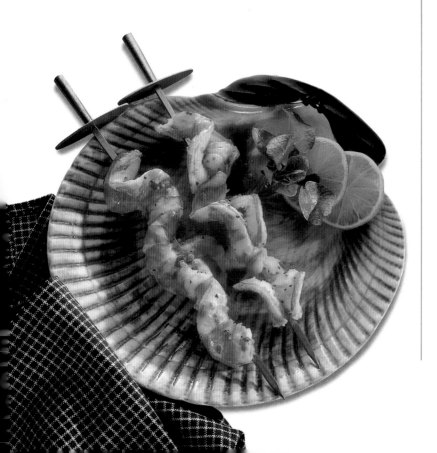

Eggs with Creamed Spinach and Hollandaise Sauce

- **25 g/1 oz butter**
- **2 large cooked artichoke bottoms**
- **4 anchovy fillets**
- **2 eggs**
- **25 g/1 oz ham, finely diced**

CREAMED SPINACH:
- **1 tablespoon butter**
- **150 g/5 oz frozen spinach, thawed and well drained**
- **1 teaspoon flour**
- **50 ml/2 fl oz double cream**
- **grated nutmeg, to taste**
- **few drops Pernod**
- **salt and freshly ground black pepper**

HOLLANDAISE SAUCE:

2 egg yolks
1 teaspoon lemon juice
pinch salt
75 g/3 oz unsalted butter, cut into small pieces

1 Put the butter in a small baking dish in a preheated oven, 150°C/300°F/Gas Mark 2, and heat until the butter has melted. Add the artichoke bottoms and turn to coat with butter. Add the anchovy fillets and ham, keeping the ingredients separate. Cover and return to the oven to heat through.

2 Meanwhile, to make the creamed spinach, melt the butter in a pan that has an ovenproof handle. Add the spinach and toss until all excess liquid has evaporated. Sprinkle the flour over and stir in well, then stir in the cream and cook until thickened. Season with nutmeg, salt and pepper, then add a few drops of Pernod. Remove from the heat, cover and keep hot in the oven.

3 To make the hollandaise sauce, put the egg yolks, lemon juice and salt in the top of a double boiler over hot water (the base of the top part should not touch the water). Use a wire whisk and beat until very thick and pale. Beat in the butter, a little at a time, allowing each piece to be absorbed before adding the next. When all the butter has been incorporated, taste and adjust the seasoning. Remove the double boiler from the heat but leave the top part over hot water to keep the sauce warm.

4 To complete the dish, poach the eggs until the whites are set but the yolks are still runny. Spoon a round of creamed spinach in the centre of four warmed plates. Place an artichoke bottom on top and spoon a little hot, softened anchovy into each. Drain the poached eggs thoroughly and place one on each artichoke bottom. Spoon over the hollandaise sauce and scatter the diced ham on top. Serve immediately.

Preparation time: 20 minutes
Cooking time: 10 minutes
Oven temperature: 150°C/300°F/Gas Mark 2

Oysters in Cream Sauce

- **12 fresh oysters in shell, opened, rinsed and liquor strained and reserved**
- **SAUCE:**
- **2 tablespoons unsalted butter**
- **2 spring onions, including green parts, chopped,**
- **1 garlic clove, crushed**
- **1 tablespoon flour**
- **50 ml/2 fl oz dry white vermouth or wine**
- **Tabasco sauce, to taste**
- **1 egg yolk**
- **50 ml/2 fl oz double cream**
- **25 g/1 oz button mushrooms, finely chopped**
- **75 g/3 oz cooked, shelled prawns, finely chopped**
- **salt and freshly ground white pepper**
- **20 g/¾ oz Parmesan cheese, grated**
- **2 tablespoons fine dry breadcrumbs**

1 Measure 250 ml/8 fl oz oyster liquor. Add dry white wine to make up the quantity. Scrub the deeper shell halves and add an oyster to each. Arrange in crumpled foil in a pan. Keep cool.

2 Melt the butter in a saucepan, then add the spring onions and garlic. Cook, stirring, until softened but not browned. Stir in the flour and continue cooking for 1 minute, then gradually stir in the oyster liquor and vermouth or wine. Bring to the boil, lower the heat and simmer for 5 minutes, stirring constantly. Season to taste, adding a little Tabasco sauce.

3 Blend the egg yolk and cream. Add 2 tablespoons of the hot sauce, then stir into the remaining sauce in the pan. Gently stir until thickened, without boiling. Remove from heat and stir in the mushrooms and prawns. Spoon over the oysters.

4 Mix together the Parmesan and breadcrumbs and sprinkle over the tops of the oysters. Bake in a preheated oven, 200°C/400°F/Gas Mark 6, for 15–20 minutes or until golden brown and the edges of the oysters begin to curl. Serve hot.

Preparation time: 15 minutes
Cooking time: 30–40 minutes
Oven temperature: 200°C/400°F/Gas Mark 6

Parma Ham with Avocado

- **1 ripe medium avocado**
- **6 slices Parma ham, about 75 g/3 oz**
- **DRESSING:**
- **1 tablespoon olive oil**
- **1 teaspoon lemon juice**
- **1 garlic clove, crushed**
- **2 teaspoons chopped fresh parsley**
- **salt and freshly ground black pepper**

1 Cut the avocado in half and remove the stone. Peel off the skin and cut each half into 3 thick slices.

2 Wrap each slice of ham around a slice of avocado. Arrange on a serving dish or individual dishes.

3 Place all the dressing ingredients in a screw-topped jar and shake well to mix together.

4 Pour the dressing over to serve.

Preparation time: 10 minutes

Timbales of Smoked Salmon

- 175 g/6 oz smoked salmon, thinly sliced
- 50 ml/2 fl oz crème fraîche, chilled
- 1 tablespoon red caviar or salmon roe, plus extra, to garnish
- pinch of cayenne or dash of Tabasco sauce, to taste

TOMATO PUREE:
- 2 ripe tomatoes, skinned, deseeded and chopped
- salt and freshly ground black pepper

to garnish:
- whole fresh chives or fresh dill

1 Rinse 2 small soufflé dishes and line with clingfilm. Line with 150 g/5 oz of the smoked salmon slices and overlap the sides. Chop the remaining salmon finely. Beat the crème fraîche until soft peaks form, and fold in the chopped salmon, caviar and cayenne pepper or Tabasco.
2 Fill the moulds, fold over the sides of overlapping salmon, cover and chill overnight.
3 To make the tomato purée, purée the tomato flesh, then rub through a fine sieve. Season with salt and pepper and chill.
4 Unmould the timbales on to individual serving plates and spoon a circle of tomato purée around each one. Garnish the top of the timbales with the chives or fresh dill.

Preparation time: 30 minutes, plus overnight chilling

Timbales of Parma Ham

Prepare the soufflé dishes as for the main recipe then substitute 175 g/6 oz thinly slice Parma ham for the smoked salmon. Beat the crème fraîche with 1 tablespoon of mascarpone cheese. Continue as for the main recipe, garnishing with extra mascarpone and whole basil leaves.

*True love's the gift which God has given
To man alone beneath the heaven.*

SIR WALTER SCOTT 1771–1832

Main
Courses

Fillet Steak with Smoked Oysters

- 300 g/10 oz beef fillet cut into 2 steaks
- 1 tablespoon soya or sunflower oil
- 50 g/2 oz onions, finely sliced
- 75 g/3 oz button mushrooms, finely sliced
- 25 ml/1 fl oz red wine
- 25 ml/1 fl oz beef stock
- 1 tablespoon tomato purée
- 50 g/2 oz canned smoked oysters, drained
- salt and freshly ground black pepper
- sprigs of watercress, to garnish

1 Carefully cut three-quarters through each steak and open out butterfly fashion. Place between 2 sheets of greaseproof paper and beat with a rolling pin to an even thickness.
2 Season and brush lightly with a little oil. Place under a preheated hot grill and cook for 6–10 minutes.
3 Meanwhile, heat the remaining oil in a pan and sauté the onions and mushrooms for a few minutes until they have softened. Add the wine, stock and tomato purée and simmer for

3–4 minutes, until the liquid is slightly reduced and the sauce thickened. Stir in the oysters.
4 Spoon over the sauce and garnish with sprigs of watercress.

Preparation time: 15 minutes
Cooking time: 15–20 minutes

Pork with Orange and Apricots

- 15 g/½ oz butter
- 2 pork chops
- grated rind and juice of ½ orange
- 1 small onion, finely chopped
- ½ green pepper, cored, deseeded and chopped
- 200 ml/7 fl oz stock
- 1 teaspoon cornflour
- pinch of sugar
- 50 g/2 oz dried apricots
- salt and freshly ground black pepper

1 Melt the butter in a frying pan. Add the chops and fry on both sides until evenly browned.
2 Transfer to a shallow ovenproof dish, using a slotted spoon. Sprinkle with the orange rind and salt and pepper to taste.
3 Add the onion and pepper to the fat remaining in the pan and fry until soft. Stir in the stock.
4 Blend the cornflour with the orange juice and add to the pan. Heat, stirring, until the sauce thickens. Add sugar and season.
5 Arrange the apricots on top of the pork and pour over the sauce. Continue to simmer for 15–20 minutes.
6 Serve hot with sauté potatoes and a selection of baby vegetables.

Preparation time: 20 minutes
Cooking time: 30–40 minutes

Tournedos en Croûte

- 25 g/1 oz butter
- 1 tablespoon oil
- 1 small onion, finely chopped
- 1 garlic clove, crushed
- 50 g/2 oz mushrooms, finely chopped
- pinch of ground nutmeg
- 2 fillet steaks, about 175 g/6 oz each, trimmed
- 125 g/4 oz fresh or frozen puff pastry

- 1 egg, beaten
- 2 slices ham
- salt and freshly ground black pepper

1 Heat half the butter and the oil in a frying pan and gently cook the onion and garlic until soft. Add the mushrooms and nutmeg, and season with salt and pepper. Stir over a gentle heat until the musrooms are cooked and the moisture has evaporated. Remove from the pan, divide into 4 portions and leave to cool.

2 Heat the remaining butter in a clean frying pan, add the fillet

steaks and then sear quickly on both sides. Remove from the pan, cool quickly and keep chilled until required.

3 Roll out the pastry on a lightly floured surface and cut into 4 rounds large enough to half-cover the steaks. Brush a 2.5 cm/1 inch border around the edge of each pastry round with beaten egg. Cut the ham into 4 rounds the same size as the steaks.

4 Place 1 piece of ham on each of 2 pastry rounds. Cover the ham with a portion of the mushroom mixture, a fillet steak, another portion of mushrooms and another round of ham. Top with a pastry circle. Seal the edges of the pastry between your fingers and then with a fork. Cut any pastry trimmings into leaves and use to decorate the croûtes. Brush with beaten egg and cook in a preheated oven, 220°C/425°F/Gas Mark 7, for 20 minutes, until golden brown. Serve with new potatoes and asparagus.

Preparation time: 20 minutes
Cooking time: 30–35 minutes
Oven temperature: 220°C/425°F/Gas Mark 7

Venison with Port and Fresh Figs

- **2 slices venison fillet or chump steaks, approximately 125–175 g/4–6 oz each**
- **75 ml/3 fl oz port**
- **25 ml/1 fl oz red wine vinegar**
- **1 teaspoon olive oil**
- **40 g/1½ oz shallots or small onions, finely sliced**
- **1 teaspoon wholemeal flour**
- **50 ml/2 fl oz beef stock**
- **2 ripe figs**
- **½ teaspoon mild mustard**
- **salt and freshly ground black pepper**

1 Trim any fat from the steaks. Place them in a shallow dish. Add the port and vinegar. Cover and refrigerate overnight.

2 Heat the oil in a large, flameproof casserole and sauté the shallots or small onions until they have softened.

3 Lift the meat out of the marinade, reserving the liquid. Add the steaks to the casserole and sauté them for about 2 minutes to seal each side. Remove the steaks.

4 Add the flour to the casserole and cook for 1 minute. Stir in the stock and the marinade. Bring to the boil, stirring. Scoop the flesh from one of the figs and add to the casserole with the mustard, salt and pepper.

5 Return the steaks to the casserole. Lower the heat, cover and simmer gently for 45 minutes, stirring occasionally, until tender. Garnish with the remaining fig, sliced. Serve with pasta.

Preparation time: 20 minutes, plus overnight marinating
Cooking time: 45 minutes

Indonesian Steak with Chilli

- **300 g/10 oz rump steak or beef topside**
- **1 teaspoon ground coriander**
- **1 tablespoon tamarind water or lime juice**
- **pinch of brown sugar**
- **4 fresh chillies, deseeded and chopped**
- **2 shallots or ½ onion, chopped**
- **2 garlic cloves, chopped**
- **3 tablespoons sunflower oil**
- **1 teaspoon lemon juice**
- **salt and freshly ground black pepper**

1 Using a sharp knife, slice the meat thinly across the grain, then cut the slices into 5 cm/2 inch squares. Arrange in a single layer on a large plate and sprinkle with the coriander, tamarind water or lime juice, sugar and salt and pepper. Press each piece of meat with your hands so that the spices and flavourings are thoroughly absorbed by the meat, then spread the slices out on the plate again. Cover with foil or clingfilm, then leave to stand for 2–3 hours in a cool place.

2 Put the chopped chillies, shallots or onion and garlic in a liquidizer or food processor and work until they are just broken down, but not reduced to a paste.

3 Heat the oil in a large heavy frying pan. Add the squares of seasoned meat and fry, stirring frequently, until evenly browned and cooked through. Remove from the pan with a slotted spoon and keep hot.

4 Add the pounded chilli mixture to the oil remaining in the pan and fry for 2–3 minutes, stirring constantly.

5 Return the meat to the pan and stir well, until coated with the chilli mixture. Add the lemon juice and salt to taste and stir well. Serve the steak hot with plain boiled rice and a selection of relishes and pickles.

Preparation time: 30 minutes, plus standing
Cooking time: 10 minutes

All love is sweet,
Given or returned.
Common as light is love,
And its familiar voice wearies not ever.

P. B. SHELLEY 1792–1822

Noisettes of Lamb with Pomegranates

- **4 noisettes of lamb**
- **½ pomegranate**
- **1 spring onion, chopped finely**
- **few black peppercorns, lightly crushed**
- **50 ml/2 fl oz rich lamb or beef stock**
- **50 ml/2 fl oz red wine**
- **sprigs of parsley, to garnish**

1 Trim any excess fat from the lamb and place the noisettes in a shallow dish, in one layer. Using a lemon squeezer, squeeze the juice from the pomegranate and pour it over the lamb. Add the spring onions and peppercorns. Cover and leave to marinate for at least 2 hours.

2 Drain the noisettes, reserving the marinade, and dry them on kitchen paper. In a non-stick pan, fry the lamb noisettes without added fat, to seal them on both sides. Pour over the stock and red wine. Simmer, uncovered, until the liquid has reduced by about half. Add the reserved marinade and bring to the boil.

3 Remove the noisettes from the pan with a slotted spoon and arrange them on a serving plate. Garnish with parsley sprigs. Pour the sauce over and serve.

Preparation time: 15 minutes, plus at least 2 hours marinating
Cooking time: 20 minutes

Roast Pheasant Flambéed with Calvados

- **1 pheasant, preferably a hen bird, plucked and cleaned ready for the oven**
- **1 small onion, halved**
- **25 g/1 oz butter**
- **2 tart dessert apples, peeled, cored and thickly sliced**

SAUCE:
- **salt and freshly ground black pepper**
- **15 g/½ oz plain flour**
- **150 ml/¼ pint dry white wine**
- **2 tablespoons Calvados**
- **50 ml/2 fl oz double cream**
- **1 tablespoon chopped fresh parsley**

1 Place the prepared pheasant in a roasting tin. Tuck the onion halves under the birds and sprinkle with a little salt and pepper. Dot with the butter and place in a preheated oven, 190°C/375°F/Gas Mark 5. Roast for about 45 minutes, or until the pheasant is cooked through and tender.

2 Add the apples to the tin 15–20 minutes before the end of the cooking time.

3 Have ready a warmed serving dish. Remove the pheasant from the roasting tin and transfer it to the dish. Place the apple slices in a separate dish and keep them hot while making the Calvados sauce.

4 Stir the flour into the pan juices and cook over a moderate heat for 1 minute. Stir in the dry white wine and bring to the boil, stirring all the time. Remove from the heat.

5 Heat the Calvados in a small saucepan until it is just warm, set it alight and then, when the flames die down, add it to the sauce. Stir in the double cream and chopped parsley and adjust the seasoning to taste, then reheat the sauce without boiling.

6 Pour a little of the sauce around the pheasant and arrange the apples in the dish. Serve the pheasant accompanied by game chips and fresh green vegetables, with the remaining sauce served separately.

Preparation time: 20 minutes
Cooking time: 45 minutes
Oven temperature: 190°C/375°F/Gas Mark 5

Lobster Thermidor

- 1 x 1 kg/2 lb lobster, cooked
- 50 g/2 oz butter
- 1 small onion, finely chopped
- 25 g/1 oz plain flour
- 150 ml/¼ pint milk
- 25 g/1 oz Cheddar cheese, grated
- 1 tablespoon white wine
- pinch of paprika pepper
- Parmesan cheese, grated
- salt and freshly ground black pepper

TO GARNISH:
- lettuce leaves
- watercress
- lemon wedges

1 Remove the lobster meat from the shell, then cut it up into pieces about 1 cm/½ inch long (you will find this easier if you cut the meat at an angle). Heat half the butter in a small frying pan and add the lobster. Fry gently, turning occasionally.
2 Meanwhile, in a small pan, heat the remaining butter. Add the onion and fry gently until soft. Add the flour and blend thoroughly.
3 Add the milk to the pan, stirring, and bring to the boil. Simmer for a few minutes, then add the Cheddar cheese. Mix thoroughly over a low heat, before adding the wine and paprika pepper. Season to taste with salt and pepper.
4 Pour the sauce over the lobster in the frying pan and mix well. Cook over a low heat for a few minutes. Place the cleaned lobster shells on a grill rack, then spoon the lobster mixture into them.
5 Sprinkle thickly with Parmesan cheese and place under a preheated grill. Cook until the sauce is bubbling and golden brown. Place on an oval platter on which you have arranged a bed of lettuce. Garnish with watercress and lemon wedges.

Preparation time: 45 minutes
Cooking time: 20 minutes

VARIATION:

Lobster with Green Goddess Dressing

FOR THE DRESSING:
1 small garlic clove, chopped
2 anchovy fillets, well drained
1 tablespoon snipped chives
1 tablespoon chopped fresh parsley
1 teaspoon chopped fresh tarragon
125 ml/4 fl oz mayonnaise
½ tablespoon tarragon vinegar
salt and black pepper
1 tablespoon crème fraîche

1 Cook the lobster as given in step one of the main recipe. Set aside to cool and arrange on a serving plate.
2 To make the dressing: put the garlic, anchovies and herbs in the bowl of a food processor and blend well. Add the mayonnaise and blend. Add the vinegar and season to taste. Transfer to a bowl, cover and refrigerate for at least 1 hour. Stir in the crème fraîche before serving.
3 Arrange salad leaves of your choice around the lobster. Spoon over a little of the dressing and serve the rest separately.

'Age cannot wither her, nor custom stale
Her infinite variety; other men cloy
The appetites they feed, but she makes hungry
Where most she satisfies'.
ANTHONY OF CLEOPATRA, ANTHONY AND CLEOPATRA

Pan-fried Salmon with Tomato Coulis

- 1 garlic clove, crushed
- 1 tablespoon olive oil
- 2 fresh salmon steaks or cutlets
- ground nutmeg, to taste
- ½ small glass claret (optional)
- salt and freshly ground black pepper

TOMATO COULIS:
- 750 g/1½ lb ripe tomatoes, sliced
- 1 small onion, finely chopped
- pinch of sugar
- bouquet garni
- juice of ½ lemon
- salt and freshly ground black pepper

1 Place all the ingredients for the tomato coulis, except the lemon juice, in a pan and bring to the boil. Reduce the heat, cover and simmer until very soft. Remove the bouquet garni.

2 Purée, then press through a sieve. Return to the boil and reduce to a sauce-like consistency. Add the lemon juice and season to taste.

3 Sauté the garlic in the oil for a few minutes and discard. Season the salmon with salt and nutmeg, add to pan, and sauté at a high heat for a few seconds on either side. Reduce the heat and cook until the fish is cooked through. Remove and keep warm. Deglaze the pan with the claret and add to the coulis.

4 Place a portion of salmon on each individual plate and spoon over the tomato coulis. Serve with mixed green leaves.

Preparation time: 20 minutes
Cooking time: 10–15 minutes

VARIATION:

Pan-fried Salmon with Crème Fraîche and Fresh Watercress

1 Sauté 1 clove of crushed garlic in 1 tablespoon olive oil for a few minutes. Discard the garlic. Season the salmon with salt and nutmeg and add to the pan. Sauté for a few seconds on either side. Reduce the heat and cook until the fish is cooked through, remove and keep warm.

2 Chop a small bunch of fresh watercress very finely and stir into about 125 ml/4 fl oz of crème fraîche and a squeeze of lemon juice.

3 Arrange the salmon on individual plates and spoon over the crème fraîche and watercress sauce. Serve with new potatoes and a salad of mixed green leaves.

Preparation time: 20 minutes
Cooking time: 10–15 minutes

Little deeds of kindness, little words of love,
Help to make earth happy, like the heaven above.

JULIA CARNEY 1823–1908

Lemon-fried Fish with Mushrooms and Mangetout

- **2 haddock fillets, skinned and cut into bite-sized pieces**
- **1 tablespoon corn oil**
- **1 tablespoon sesame oil**
- **125 g/4 oz oyster mushrooms, sliced**
- **125 g/4 oz mangetout**
- **few sprigs of flat-leaf parsley, to garnish**

MARINADE:
- **1 small piece fresh root ginger, peeled and finely chopped**
- **1 garlic clove, crushed**
- **3 teaspoons soy sauce**
- **finely grated rind and juice of ½ lemon**
- **pinch of five-spice powder**

1 To make the marinade, place the ginger and garlic in a shallow dish with the soy sauce, lemon rind, lemon juice and five-spice powder and mix together.

2 Add the pieces of fish to the dish and turn to coat thoroughly in the marinade. Cover the dish and leave to marinate for about 30 minutes, turning the fish over occasionally.

3 Heat a wok or large skillet until hot. Add half the corn and sesame oils and heat over a moderate heat until hot. Add the sliced mushrooms and mangetout, and stir-fry for 3–4 minutes. Tip the contents of the wok or skillet into a bowl and set aside.

4 Return the wok or skillet to the heat, add the remaining corn and sesame oils and heat until hot. With a slotted spoon, lift the fish out of the marinade and place carefully in the pan.

5 Stir-fry the fish for 5 minutes, then return the mushrooms and mangetout to the pan with their juices and pour in the marinade.

6 Increase the heat to high and gently toss until all the incredients are well combined and piping hot. Serve at once, garnished with sprigs of flat-leaf parsley.

Preparation time: 10 minutes, plus 30 minutes marinating
Cooking time: 10 minutes

There's nothing half so sweet in life
As love's young dream.

THOMAS MOORE 1779–1852

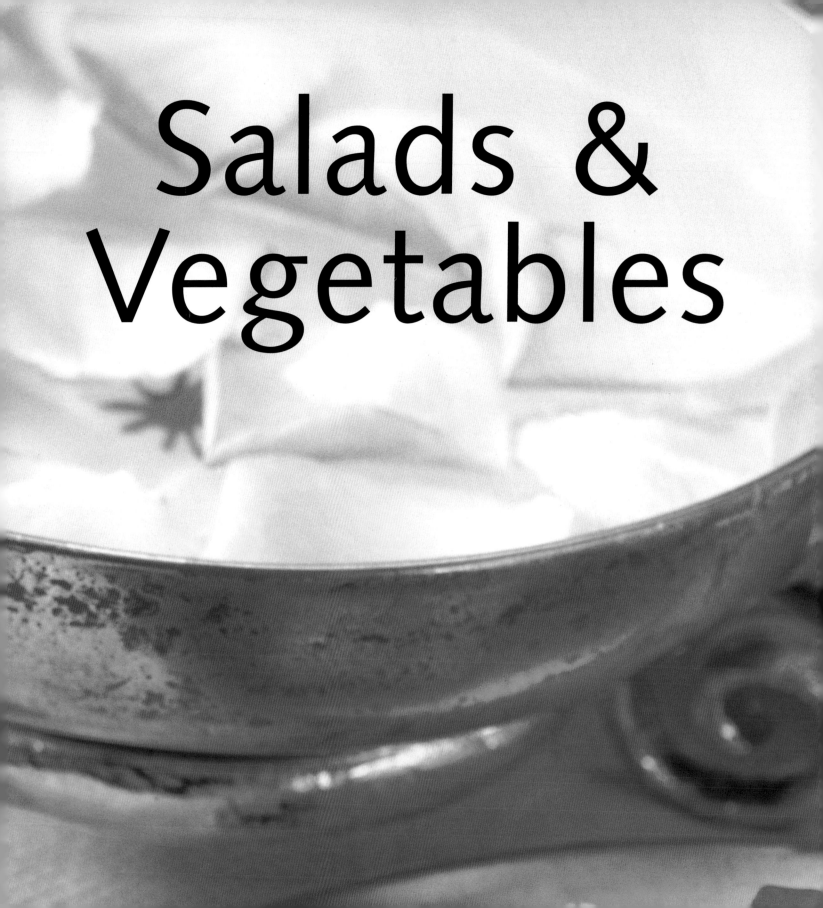

Salads & Vegetables

Spicy Crab Salad

• **large lettuce leaves**
• **Chinese leaves, shredded**
• **250 g/8 oz crabmeat**
• **2 tomatoes, cut into wedges**
• **2 hard-boiled eggs, cut into wedges**
DRESSING:
• **125 ml/4 fl oz mayonnaise**
• **50 ml/2 fl oz chilli sauce**
• **2 spring onions, chopped**
• **I tablespoon chopped fresh parsley**
• **I teaspoon tomato purée**
• **dash Worcestershire sauce**
• **50 ml/2 fl oz double cream, whipped**
• **salt and freshly ground black pepper**

I First make the dressing: Combine the mayonnaise, chilli sauce, spring onions, parsley, tomato purée and Worcestershire sauce in a bowl, and season to taste. Stir well to mix, then fold in the whipped cream. Cover and refrigerate for at least 1 hour.
2 Line a serving platter with the lettuce leaves and make an even layer of shredded Chinese leaves in the centre. Pile the crabmeat on top. Arrange the tomato and egg wedges around the crabmeat. Spoon some of the dressing over the crab and serve the rest separately.

Preparation time: 15 minutes, plus 1 hour chilling

VARIATION:
For a less spicy version of this dish, prepare the salad as given in the main recipe and serve with delicious home-made mayonnaise.

Mayonnaise

• **2 eggs yolks**
• **I tablespoon white wine vinegar or tarragon vinegar**
• **I teaspoon Dijon mustard**
• **300 ml/½ pint olive oil**
• **salt and pepper**

I Put the egg yolks in a bowl with the vinegar and mustard. Add $1/2$ teaspoon of salt and some pepper. Beat to a smooth paste.
2 Gradually beat in the oil, adding 1 drop at a time at first. When the mixture thickens, pour the oil in a steady stream, beating until all the oil has been added and the mayonnaise is thick.
3 Alternatively, put the egg yolks, vinegar, mustard, salt and pepper in a blender or food processor. Process briefly, then add the oil, drop by drop at first, then in a steady stream until the oil has been incorporated and the mayonnaise is thick. Put in a bowl and use as indicated in recipes.

Makes about 325 ml/11 fl oz
Preparation time: 10-15 minutes

Lobster and Asparagus Salad with Herb Dressing

Preparation time: 20 minutes
Cooking time: 45 minutes

- **500 g/1 lb asparagus spears**
- **2 lobsters, approximately 500–750 g/1–1½ lb each, freshly cooked**
- **mixed salad leaves, to serve**

HERB DRESSING:
- **1 small garlic clove, crushed**
- **2 anchovies, well drained**
- **1 tablespoon snipped fresh chives**
- **1 tablespoon chopped fresh parsley**
- **1 teaspoon chopped fresh tarragon**
- **125 ml/4 fl oz mayonnaise**
- **1 teaspoon tarragon vinegar**
- **few tablespoons soured cream (optional)**
- **salt and freshly ground black pepper**

1 First make the dressing: put the garlic, anchovy fillets and herbs in a food processor and process until well blended. Add the mayonnaise and process to mix. Add the vinegar and seasoning to taste. Pour and scrape into a bowl, cover and refrigerate for at least 1 hour. Before serving, stir in a few tablespoons of soured cream, if liked.

2 Trim the woody ends from the asparagus spears, making the spears the same length. Then, if necessary, scrape the sides of each spear with a swivel-bladed vegetable parer, starting about 5 cm/2 inches from the tip. Cook the asparagus in a pan of boiling salted water for 4–8 minutes, depending on size, or until tender but still crisp. Drain and refresh under cold running water, then drain again. Leave to cool.

3 Crack the claws and tails of the lobsters and remove the meat. Keep the claw meat whole, and slice the tail meat across into neat rounds.

4 Arrange the asparagus spears and lobster meat on a bed of salad leaves. Spoon over a little of the dressing and serve the rest separately.

VARIATION:

Lobster and Asparagus Salad with Aïoli

Aïoli is a Provençal variation on mayonnaise, strongly flavoured with garlic.

Prepare the asparagus and lobster as given in the main recipe and arrange on a bed of salad leaves

TO MAKE THE AÏOLI:
Make a basic mayonnaise (see page 42). Put the mayonnaise in a bowl and stir in 2 crushed garlic cloves. Leave the aïoli to stand for at least 30 minutes before serving. Spoon a little over the lobster and asparagus and serve the rest separately.

Preparation time: 20 minutes
Cooking time: 45 minutes plus standing

Drink to me only with thine eyes,
And I will pledge with mine;
Or leave a kiss but in the cup,
And I'll not look for wine.

BEN JOHNSON 1572-1637 (TO CELIA)

Oyster Mushroom Salad

- 125 g/4 oz baby button mushrooms, halved
- 50 g/2 oz oyster mushrooms
- 75 ml/3 fl oz French dressing
- 2 tablespoons chopped fresh mint
- 125 g/4 oz tiny cherry tomatoes, halved

1 Put all the mushrooms in a dish. Combine the French dressing with the chopped mint and pour it over the mushrooms. Cover the dish tightly and leave to marinate for at least 3–4 hours, turning occasionally.
2 Drain the excess dressing (but not the mint) and arrange the mushrooms in a serving bowl. Add the tomatoes and serve.

Preparation time: 10 minutes plus marinating

Carrots with Ginger and Almonds

- 25–40 g/1–1½ oz flaked almonds
- 1 tablespoon sunflower oil
- ½ onion, sliced
- 2.5 cm/1 inch piece of fresh root ginger, peeled and cut into matchsticks
- 175 g/6 oz young carrots, cut into matchsticks
- 2 tablespoons vegetable stock or water
- 1 tablespoon sweet sherry
- salt and freshly ground black pepper

1 Heat a wok or large frying pan until hot. Add the almonds and dry-fry over a gentle heat, stirring frequently, until golden brown on all sides. Remove from the pan and set aside.
2 Add the oil to the pan and place over a moderate heat. When the oil is hot, add the onion and ginger and stir-fry for 2–3 minutes or until softened, taking care not to let them brown.
3 Add the carrots, stock or water, sherry and salt and pepper to taste. Increase the heat to high and stir-fry for 3–4 minutes or until the carrots are just tender and the liquid has evaporated. Adjust the seasoning to taste and serve, sprinkled with the almonds.

Preparation time: 10 minutes
Cooking time: 5–7 minutes

Melon and Celery Salad

- ½ small melon
- ½ celery heart
- 2 tablespoons vinaigrette
- I teaspoon grated fresh ginger or pinch ground ginger
- lettuce or endive
- 2 tablespoons chopped walnuts

I Remove the seeds from the melon and cut the pulp into neat balls, using a melon baller or vegetable scoop. Neatly dice the celery.
2 Blend the vinaigrette with the ginger and leave the celery in this until ready to serve the salad. Arrange the melon and celery on the lettuce or endive and top with chopped walnuts.

Preparation time: 10 minutes

Avocado and Grapefruit Salad

- I pink grapefruit
- I small avocado
- I tablespoon sunflower oil
- I teaspoon lemon juice or to taste
- I teaspoon sugar, or to taste
- salt and freshly ground black pepper
TO GARNISH:
- lettuce leaves
- chopped parsley

I Cut away the peel from the grapefruit, then cut out the segments. Do this over a basin so that the juice can be used in the dressing.
2 Skin, stone and slice the avocado.
3 Add the oil, lemon juice, sugar and seasoning to the grapefruit juice. Keep the avocado in this until just before serving the salad.

4 Arrange alternate slices of grapefruit and avocado on a serving plate and serve with a garnish of lettuce leaves and chopped parsley.

Preparation time: 10–15 minutes

Hawaiian Salad

- **I bunch of spring onions**
- **3 tablespoons rice vinegar**
- **I tablespoon sugar, plus I teaspoon**
- **2 tablespoons olive oil**
- **I tablespoon lime juice**
- **pinch of dried mustard**
- **125 g/4 oz smoked salmon, thinly sliced**
- **50 g/2 oz diced tomatoes**
- **salt and freshly ground black pepper**
- **shredded spinach leaves, to serve**

I Trim off the green tops of the spring onions to make them 10 cm/4 inches long, but leave the root ends intact. Sprinkle the spring onions liberally with salt, then roll and knead them until they feel soft and limp. Keep sprinkling with salt as you knead. Rinse the spring onions well and dry on paper towels.

2 Combine 2 tablespoons of the vinegar and 1 tablespoon of sugar in a small shallow bowl and stir to dissolve the sugar. Add the spring onions. Cover and leave to marinate in a cool place for at least 1 hour, turning them over occasionally.

3 Meanwhile, mix together the remaining vinegar and sugar with the oil, lime juice and mustard in another shallow bowl, and season to taste. Add 1 slice of salmon, turning it to coat with dressing on both sides, and pat and massage it gently to mix in the dressing. Remove and set aside. Continue dressing and massaging the slices of salmon 1 at a time. When all have been dressed, put them back in the bowl. Cover and leave to marinate at cool room temperature, or in the refrigerator, for at least 1 hour.

4 Drain the salmon, reserving the dressing, and cut it into strips. Put the strips back in the bowl with the dressing.

5 Drain the spring onions and cut crosswise into 5 mm–1 inch/$^1/_4$–$^1/_2$ inch pieces. Add to the salmon with the tomatoes and toss together gently.

6 Make a bed of shredded spinach on a serving platter and pile the salmon salad on top.

Preparation time: 1 hour, including marinating

Desserts

Banana and Coconut Tart

- **200 g/7 oz plain flour**
- **pinch of salt**
- **100 g/3½ oz butter**
- **3 tablespoons cold water**

FILLING:
- **7 tablespoons milk**
- **75 g/3 oz caster sugar**
- **100 g/3½ oz desiccated coconut**
- **2 eggs, beaten**
- **1 tablespoon rum**
- **5 bananas, sliced**
- **juice of 1 lemon**

SYRUP:
- **1 tablespoon rum**
- **4 tablespoons sugar**

TO DECORATE:
- **150 ml/¼ pint double cream, whipped**
- **8 maraschino cherries**

1 To make the pastry, sift the flour and salt into a bowl. Dice the butter into the flour and rub in, then mix to a dough with the cold water. Roll out the dough on a floured surface and line a buttered 22 cm/8½ inch flan dish.
2 Prick the base lightly with a fork and bake blind in a preheated moderately hot oven, 200°C/400°F/Gas Mark 6, for about 15 minutes, until the pastry has begun to form a slight crust. Remove the foil from the pastry and continue to bake for a further 10 minutes until completely baked.
3 To make the filling, boil the milk in a small pan and leave to cool slightly. Mix together the sugar and the coconut, then stir in the beaten eggs. Add the milk, stirring, then return to the pan and thicken over a low heat, stirring constantly. Add the rum and cool.
4 Toss the banana in the lemon juice, strain and reserve it.
5 In another small pan, mix the rum, sugar and the strained lemon juice from the bananas. Heat the mixture over a low heat until the sugar dissolves, then boil to form a thick syrup. Pour the coconut mixture into the pastry case. Arrange the bananas over the top and pour over the syrup. Decorate with whipped cream and the cherries.

Makes a 22 cm/8½ inch flan
Preparation time: 30 minutes, plus cooling
Cooking time: 45 minutes
Oven temperature: 200°C/400°F/Gas Mark 6

Exotic Fruit Salad

- **1 small pineapple**
- **1 passion fruit**
- **1 kiwi fruit, peeled and sliced**
- **1 mango, peeled and sliced, stone removed**
- **3 tablespoons Kirsch**

1 Cut the top off the pineapple and pull away 2 or 3 leaves.
2 Cut out the flesh of the pineapple by cutting around it with a long sharp knife and scooping out the flesh with a spoon.
3 Slice the flesh into bite-sized pieces, discarding the core.
4 Halve the passion fruit and spoon out the flesh.
5 Mix all the fruits together in a bowl with the Kirsch. Spoon them into the pineapple shell and chill.
6 Just before serving, decorate with the pineapple leaves. Serve with plain unsweetened yogurt or pouring cream.

Preparation time: 30 minutes, plus cooling

Chestnut Roulade

- **3 eggs, separated**
- **125 g/4 oz caster sugar**
- **1 x 250 g/8 oz can unsweetened chestnut purée**
- **grated rind and juice of 1 orange**
- **sieved icing sugar, for sprinkling**
- **300 ml/½ pint double cream**
- **2 tablespoons Grand Marnier**

1 Whisk the egg yolks with the sugar until thick and creamy. Put the chestnut purée in a bowl with the orange juice and beat until blended, then whisk into the egg mixture. Whisk the egg whites until fairly stiff and fold in carefully. Turn into a greased and lined 30 x 20 cm/12 x 8 inch Swiss roll tin. Bake in a preheated oven, 180°C/350°F/Gas Mark 4, for 25–30 minutes, until firm.

2 Cool for 5 minutes, then cover with a damp tea towel and leave until cold. Carefully turn the roulade on to a sheet of greaseproof paper sprinkled thickly with icing sugar. Peel off the lining paper.

3 Place the cream, grated orange rind and Grand Marnier in a bowl and whip until stiff. Spread over the roulade and roll up like a Swiss roll. Transfer to a serving dish.

Makes enough for a 30 x 20 cm/12 x 8 inch Swiss roll tin
Preparation time: 25 minutes
Cooking time: 25–30 minutes
Oven temperature: 180°C/350°F/Gas Mark 4

Strawberry Shortbread Creams

- **125 g/4 oz butter**
- **175 g/6 oz plain flour**
- **50 g/2 oz caster sugar**
- **grated rind of 1 orange**

FILLING:
- **150 ml/¼ pint double or whipping cream**
- **250 g/8 oz strawberries, halved**

1 Grease a 20 cm/8 inch fluted flan ring and a baking tray. Rub the butter into the flour. Add the sugar and orange rind, knead the mixture together until it forms a soft dough.

2 Turn out on to a lightly floured surface and roll to a circle large enough to fill the flan ring. Place in the flan ring on the baking tray, press into the fluted edges and smooth the top. Prick all over with a fork and mark into 8 equal portions.

3 Bake in a moderate oven, 180°C/350°F/Gas Mark 4, for 45–50 minutes. Leave to cool in the ring for 10 minutes, cut into 8.

4 Whip the cream until stiff. Spoon or pipe the cream on to four pieces of shortbread, add the strawberries to the cream and top with a second piece of shortbread.

Makes 4
Preparation time: 20 minutes
Cooking time: 45–50 minutes
Oven temperature: 180°C/350°F/Gas Mark 4

Strawberry Meringue Heart

- **450 ml/¾ pint double cream, whipped**
- **250 g/8 oz fresh strawberries**
- **NUT MERINGUE:**
- **4 egg whites**
- **250 g/8 oz caster sugar**
- **few drops vanilla essence**
- **½ teaspoon lemon juice**
- **125 g/4 oz ground almonds**

1 Line 2 baking sheets with lightly greased greaseproof paper and draw a 23 cm/9 inch wide heart on each.
2 Make the nut meringue, whisk the egg whites until stiff, then add the sugar 1 tablespoon at a time, whisking continuously until the mixture holds its shape. Gently fold in the vanilla essence, lemon juice and ground almonds.
3 Spoon the nut meringue into a piping bag fitted with a large star nozzle. Pipe heart shapes on to the paper, following the line. Working inwards, pipe smaller and smaller hearts to make a solid base. Bake in a preheated oven, 180°C/350°F/Gas Mark 4, for about 40–45 minutes, until crisp and lightly coloured, then cool.
4 Sandwich the hearts together with ²/₃ of the cream and half the strawberries. Use the remaining cream and strawberries to decorate.

5 Pipe cream rosettes around the edge of the heart and decorate with strawberries.

Preparation time: 45 minutes, plus cooling
Cooking time: 40–45 minutes

Red Fruit Salad with Coeurs à la Crème

- **375 g/12 oz raspberries**
- **2 tablespoons clear honey**
- **125 g/4 oz dessert cherries, pitted**
- **125 g/4 oz blackcurrants, stripped from stalks**
- **CURD CHEESE:**
- **1 teaspoon gelatine crystals**
- **1 tablespoon hot water**
- **175 g/6 oz cottage cheese, sieved**
- **75 ml/3 fl oz plain natural yogurt**
- **2 tablespoons double cream**
- **grated nutmeg**

1 First make the curd cheese. Sprinkle the gelatine on the water in a small bowl. Stir well and stand the bowl in hot water to dissolve the crystals.
2 Beat together the cottage cheese, yogurt and cream, then stir in the dissolved gelatine.
3 Spoon the mixture into 2 heart-shaped draining moulds. Leave overnight.
4 Liquidize half the raspberries, then sieve them. Stir the honey into the purée over a low heat. Stir in the remaining raspberries, the cherries and blackcurrants and simmer for 2–3 minutes. Cool, then chill in the refrigerator for at least 1 hour.
5 Turn out the curd cheese moulds and decorate them with a pinch of grated nutmeg. Serve them with the fruit salad as a 'sauce'.

Preparation time: 30 minutes, plus overnight draining and chilling
Cooking time: 5 minutes

Brown Bread and Chocolate Chip Ice Cream

- **600 ml/1 pint double cream**
- **1 tablespoon caster sugar**
- **125 g/4 oz fresh brown breadcrumbs**
- **75 g/3 oz soft dark brown sugar**
- **50 g/2 oz hazelnuts, chopped and toasted**
- **125 g/4 oz bitter dessert or plain chocolate, roughly chopped**

1 Turn the freezer to the fast freeze setting, or the refrigerator to its coldest setting.

2 Whip the cream with the caster sugar until it holds its shape on the whisk. Transfer to a freezer tray or a lidded container so that it can be beaten easily.

3 Freeze the cream for 30 minutes, beat thoroughly, then freeze again for a further 30 minutes.

4 Meanwhile, spread the breadcrumbs on the grill pan and sprinkle the sugar over the top. Place under a preheated grill until the sugar caramelizes. Stir well to ensure even browning. Allow to cool.

5 If necessary, grind or crush the breadcrumbs to break down any lumps. Stir in the hazelnuts.

6 Remove the frozen cream from the freezer and beat thoroughly. Stir in the breadcrumb mixture and lastly the chopped chocolate. Mix well, then return to the freezer for a further 2 hours.

7 If the ice cream has been frozen for 24 hours or longer, remove from the freezer and allow to soften for 1 hour before serving.

Makes: 600ml/1 pint
Preparation time: about 20 minutes, plus freezing

VARIATION:

Brown Bread and Blackcurrant ice cream

For a less luxurious but equally delicious ice cream the chocolate chips can be replaced by fresh blackcurrants.

1 Make the ice cream according to the instructions in the recipe.

2 Prepare 125 g/4 oz of fresh blackcurrants and poach gently in water to cover. If liked add 50 g/2 oz caster sugar to the water. When the fruit is slightly softened remove from the heat and leave to cool. Remove the fruit with a slotted spoon and drain, reserving the blackcurrant syrup.

3 Stir the blackcurrants into the frozen cream after adding the breadcrumb mixture.

4 Serve the blackcurrant syrup separately or pour a little on the side of the dish.

Makes 600ml/1 pint
Preparation time: about 25 minutes, plus freezing

And all for love and nothing for reward
EDMUND SPENSER 1522-1599

Hot Chocolate Liqueur Soufflé

- **50 g/2 oz butter, plus extra for greasing**
- **50 g/2 oz caster sugar, plus extra for sprinkling**
- **50 g/2 oz plain flour**
- **300 ml/½ pint milk**
- **75 g/3 oz plain dark or white chocolate, broken into pieces**
- **2 tablespoons Crème de Menthe**
- **3 eggs, separated**
- **I egg white**
- **50 g/2 oz caster sugar**
- **icing sugar, for dusting**
- **SAUCE:**
- **150 ml/¼ pint double cream**
- **50 g/2 oz plain dark or white chocolate, broken into pieces**
- **2 tablespoons Crème de Menthe**
- **I egg yolk**

I Butter an 18 cm/7 inch soufflé dish and dust with the sugar.
2 Combine the butter, flour and milk in a medium saucepan. Stirring continuously, heat gently until boiling. Stir vigorously until a thick paste is formed. Cook for 2–3 minutes, still stirring.

3 Away from the heat, add the chocolate and stir until smooth and completely blended into the mixture.
4 Beat in the liqueur and egg yolks.
5 Whisk the 4 egg whites until very stiff, then add the sugar. Whisk again until very stiff and, using a metal spoon, fold the chocolate mixture into the egg whites, taking care not to knock the air out of the whites.
6 Pour the soufflé mixture into the prepared soufflé dish and bake in a preheated oven, 180°C/350°F/Gas Mark 4, for 45–50 minutes, until well risen. Do not open the oven door.
7 To make the sauce, pour the cream into a small saucepan and add the chocolate. Heat gently, stirring constantly until the chocolate has melted and is thoroughly smooth. Do not boil. Stir in the liqueur and egg yolk. Pour into a jug.
8 To serve, dust the soufflé with icing sugar and take it directly from the oven to a heatproof mat on the table. Serve the soufflé with the sauce.

Preparation time: 20 minutes
Cooking time: 45 minutes–1 hour
Oven temperature: 180°C/350°F/Gas Mark 4

Chocolate and Cinnamon Bread and Butter Pudding

- **4 slices of bread from a large loaf, crusts removed**
- **25 g/I oz butter, softened**
- **I teaspoon ground cinnamon**
- **40 g/1½ oz sugar**
- **3 eggs**
- **600 ml/I pint milk**
- **I teaspoon instant coffee powder or granules**
- **75 g/3 oz plain chocolate, grated**

I Spread the sliced bread with the butter and sprinkle with the cinnamon. Cut each slice into 4 triangles.

2 Beat the sugar and eggs together in a mixing bowl. Heat the milk, coffee and half the chocolate to blood temperature. Whisk until well blended, then pour over the eggs. Mix well.
3 Layer the bread in a lightly greased 900 ml/1½ pint pie dish and strain over the custard. Stand for at least 30 minutes.
4 Place in a bain-marie, pour about 900 ml/1½ pints water around the dish and bake in a preheated oven, 180°C/350°F/Gas Mark 4, for 1¼–1½ hours, or until the custard is set. About 10 minutes before the end of the cooking time, sprinkle over the remaining chocolate.

Preparation time: 10 minutes, plus standing
Cooking time: 1¼–1½ hours
Oven temperature: 180°C/350°F/Gas Mark 4

Chocolate Hearts

- **35 g/1½ oz plain chocolate, broken into pieces**
- **125 g/4 oz low-fat soft cheese, sieved if necessary**
- **1 tablespoon caster sugar**
- **grated rind and juice of 1 orange**
- **1 teaspoon powdered gelatine**
- **65 ml/2½ fl oz whipping cream**
- **75 ml/⅛ pint single cream, to serve**
- **fresh orange segments, to serve**

1 Place the chocolate in a heatproof bowl and set over a saucepan of hot water to melt. Stir until smooth.
2 Away from the heat, gradually spoon the cheese into the chocolate, beating well between each addition. Add the sugar and orange rind.

3 Place the orange juice in a small heatproof bowl and sprinkle over the gelatine. Set the bowl over the pan of hot water and stir until dissolved. Cool slightly, then add to the cheese mixture. Chill until on the point of setting, about 30 minutes.
4 Whip the cream and fold in to the mixture. Line 2 individual heart-shaped moulds with fine muslin and divide the mixture equally between them. Smooth and chill until set, about 2 hours.
5 Carefully unmould the hearts on to a serving dish and peel off the muslin. Decorate each heart with cream, and serve with fresh orange segments.

Preparation time: 15 minutes, plus cooling and setting

Chocolate Fruity Fondue

- **50 g/2 oz milk chocolate**
- **25 g/2 oz plain chocolate**
- **1 tablespoon double cream**
- **1 teaspoon rum**
- **TO SERVE:**
- **selection of fruit, including strawberries, raspberries, cherries, sliced banana**
- **sponge fingers or langues de chat**

1 Break the milk and plain chocolate into a heatproof bowl and add the cream. Place over a saucepan of gently simmering water. Stir until the chocolate has melted.
2 Stir in the rum and continue to heat for 1 minute, stirring.
3 Pour the sauce into a warmed heatproof bowl. Serve with a selection of fruit and biscuits for dipping, using bamboo skewers to spear the fruit.

Preparation time: 20 minutes
Cooking time: 10 minutes

Passionfruit Sorbet

- **10 passionfruit**
- **juice of ½ lime**
- **100 ml/4 fl oz water**
- **300 ml/½ pint prepared Sorbet Syrup**
- **1 egg white**
- **1 teaspoon caster sugar**

SORBET SYRUP:
- **300 g/10 oz sugar**
- **300 ml/½ pint water**

1 First prepare the sorbet syrup. Place the sugar and water in a pan. Heat to boiling point, stirring continuously to dissolve the sugar. Allow to cool.

2 Scoop the flesh out of the passionfruit. Liquidize with the lime juice and water for about 10 seconds. Strain the juice into a freezer container and combine with the sorbet syrup.

3 Place the freezer container in the freezer and freeze for 2–3 hours or until almost solid.

4 Whisk the egg white and caster sugar until stiff.

5 Remove the sorbet from the freezer and beat in the egg white. Return the sorbet to the freezer for 1–2 hours or until quite set.

6 If the sorbet has been in the freezer for 24 hours or longer, transfer to the refrigerator 15 minutes before serving to soften slightly.

Preparation time: 25 minutes, plus cooling and freezing

Champagne Sorbet

- **75 g/3 oz caster sugar**
- **50 ml/2 fl oz water**
- **150 ml/¼ pint pink champagne**
- **1 tablespoon lemon juice**
- **1 egg white**
- **1 teaspoon icing sugar**

1 Dissolve the sugar in the water in a saucepan over a low heat, then bring to the boil. Boil for about 5 minutes or until the syrup is thick but not beginning to brown. Cool, then stir in a little more than half the champagne and the lemon juice. Pour into freezer trays and freeze for about 1 hour or until mushy.

2 Pour the mixture into a bowl and beat well for 2 minutes. Return to the freezer tray and freeze for a further 30 minutes. Beat again. Repeat the freezing and beating every 30 minutes for the next 2 hours.

3 Beat the egg white until stiff. Gradually beat in the icing sugar. Beat the frozen mixture well to break down the ice crystals, then fold in the meringue. Return to the freezer and freeze until firm.

4 About 30 minutes before required, transfer the sorbet to the refrigerator to soften slightly. Before serving, pour a little of the remaining champagne over each portion.

Preparation time: about 25 minutes, plus freezing
Cooking time: about 5 minutes

Cranberry Sorbet

- **200g/7oz cranberries**
- **300 ml/½ pint sorbet syrup (see page 64)**
- **100 ml/3½ fl oz orange juice**

1 Poach the cranberries in the sorbet syrup for 15 minutes. Cool slightly, then blend the cranberries, syrup and orange juice to a purée.

2 Strain the purée into a freezer container, then place in the freezer. Freeze for 2-3 hours or until almost solid.

3 Remove from the freezer and beat thoroughly to break down the ice crystals.

4 Return to the freezer for 1-2 hours or completely set.

5 If the sorbet has been in the freezer for 24 hours or longer, transfer to the refrigerator for 15 minutes before serving to soften slightly.

Preparation time: 15 minutes pus freezing
Cooking time: 15 minutes

Apple Sorbet

- **75 ml/3 fl oz dry white wine**
- **25 g/1 oz soft light brown sugar**
- **small strip of thinly pared lemon rind**
- **1 tablespoon lemon juice**
- **small piece of fresh root ginger, peeled**
- **250 g/8 oz cooking apples, peeled, cored and sliced**
- **1 egg white**
- **2 small herb leaves such as lemon geranium, to decorate**

1 Put the wine, sugar, lemon rind and juice and ginger into a saucepan and stir over a low heat until the sugar dissolves. Increase the heat and bring to the boil. Add the apple slices and poach them for 8–10 minutes, or until soft. Remove from the heat and leave to cool.
2 Discard the lemon rind and ginger and purée the fruit in a liquidizer or food processor, or rub through a sieve. Pour into a freezer container, cover and freeze for 1 hour.
3 Beat the egg white until stiff. Turn the frozen mixture into a chilled bowl and beat it to break down the ice crystals. Fold in the egg white.
4 Return the mixture to the freezer for 3–4 hours, until firm.
5 To serve, transfer the sorbet to the refrigerator for 30 minutes, scoop out and decorate with the herb leaves.

Preparation time: 20 minutes, plus freezing
Cooking time: 10–12 minutes

VARIATION:

Pear Sorbet

- **75 ml/3 fl oz red wine**
- **25 g/1 oz soft light brown sugar**
- **small strip of thinly pared lemon rind**
- **1 tablespoon lemon juice**
- **1 stick cinnamon**
- **250 g/8 oz dessert pears, peeled, cored and sliced**
- **1 egg white**

1 Put the wine, sugar, lemon rind and juice and cinnamon into a saucepan and stir over a low heat until the sugar dissolves. Increase the heat and bring to the boil. Add the pear slices and poach them for 8–10 minutes, or until soft. Remove from the heat and leave to cool.
2 Discard the lemon rind and cinnamon and purée the fruit in a liquidizer or food processor, or rub through a sieve. Pour into a freezer container, cover and freeze for 1 hour.
3 Beat the egg white until stiff. Turn the frozen mixture into a chilled bowl and beat it to break down the ice crystals. Fold in the egg white.
4 Return the mixture to the freezer for 3–4 hours, until firm.
5 To serve, transfer the sorbet to the refrigerator for 30 minutes, scoop out and serve.

Preparation time: 20 minutes, plus freezing
Cooking time: 10–12 minutes

Cakes & Biscuits

Sweetheart Cake

- **250 g/8 oz caster sugar**
- **250 g/8 oz soft margarine**
- **4 eggs**
- **250 g/8 oz self-raising flour**
- **2 teaspoons baking powder**
- **finely grated rind of 1 lemon**
- **3 tablespoons raspberry jam**
- **1½ quantities bought fondant moulding paste**
- **few drops of red food colouring**
- **icing sugar and cornflour, for dredging**
TO DECORATE:
- **royal icing for piping**
- **fresh rose buds**

1 Grease and line a 23–25 cm/9–10 inch heart-shaped tin with greased greaseproof paper or non-stick silicone paper.
2 Place the sugar, margarine, eggs, flour, baking powder and lemon rind in a mixing bowl. Beat to combine the ingredients, then beat for a further 2 minutes until the mixture is light and fluffy. Turn the mixture into the prepared tin, making sure that it is filled right to the edge. Smooth the top.
3 Place in a preheated oven, 160°C/325°F/Gas Mark 3, and bake for 45–55 minutes, until the sponge is golden brown and firm to the touch. Turn out on a wire rack, remove the lining paper and leave to cool before icing.
4 Split the cake in half horizontally and sandwich together with raspberry jam.
5 Tint the moulding paste pink with a drop or two of red food colouring. Roll out the paste on a work surface or a sheet of polythene dredged with a mixture of icing sugar and cornflour. Dredge the rolling pin with the same mixture. Roll to the width of the top of the cake, plus the sides, plus about 2.5 cm/1 inch extra.
6 Support the moulding paste on the rolling pin and place it centrally over the top of the cake. Press the moulding paste on to the sides of the cake and down the sides, using a gentle circular movement to give an even covering. Dip your fingers in the mixture of icing sugar and cornflour while you work. When the finish is smooth, trim the base edge of the cake with a sharp

knife. Place on a cake board and leave to dry for 24 hours.
7 Place two-thirds of the royal icing in a greaseproof paper piping bag fitted with a small star nozzle and pipe a border round the top and base borders of the cake, if liked. Tint the remaining icing pink with a drop of red food colouring and overpipe the base border, if liked (not shown). Decorate with fresh rose buds.

Makes a 23–25 cm/9–10 inch cake
Preparation time: 35 minutes, plus setting time
Cooking time: 45–55 minutes
Oven temperature: 160°C/325°F/Gas Mark 3

Let him kiss me with the kisses of his mouth:
for thy love is better than wine

1:2 SONG OF SOLOMAN

Lipstick Biscuits

- **50 g/2 oz caster sugar**
- **50 g/2 oz butter, softened**
- **I egg yolk**
- **125 g/4 oz plain flour, sifted**
- **pinch of salt**

GLACÉ ICING:

- **I–I½ tablespoons warm water**
- **125 g/4 oz icing sugar, sifted**
- **red food colouring**
- **2 tablespoons coloured sugar crystals**

I To make a cardboard tempate to use as a cutting guide for the biscuits, cut an oblong of cardboard 5 x 10 cm/2 x 4 inches. Draw a pair of lips to fill the cardboard and cut out the shape.

2 Cream together the sugar and butter in a mixing bowl until light and fluffy, then beat in the egg yolk.

3 Work in the flour and salt, and knead until smooth. Turn on to a lightly floured surface and roll out to a thickness of 5 mm/¼ inch.

4 Using the cardboard tempate as a guide, cut out lip shapes and place on a greased baking sheet. Re-roll the trimmings to make more biscuits.

5 Bake in a preheated oven, 200°C/400°F/Gas Mark 6, for 10–12 minutes. Allow to cool.

6 To make the glacé icing, beat sufficient warm water into the icing sugar to make a thick, smooth icing. Add enough food colouring to turn the mixture a deep red.

7 Spread the icing over the biscuits and sprinkle over the sugar crystals. Leave to set for 2 hours.

8 Pack into boxes and tie with ribbon. Freeze for up to 3 months. Thaw for 3 hours at room temperature, and decorate.

Makes about 12
Preparation time: 1 hour, plus 2 hours setting
Cooking time: 10–12 minutes
Oven temperature: 200°C/400°F/Gas Mark 6

Heart Biscuits

- **150 g/5 oz plain flour, plus extra for dusting**
- **75 g/3 oz soft butter or block margarine**
- **1 egg yolk**
- **75 g/3 oz carrots, finely grated**
- **caster sugar or icing sugar, for sprinkling**

1 Sieve the flour into a bowl and rub in the butter or margarine.

2 Add the egg yolks and carrots and work together with the hands to make a smooth dough.

3 Roll out the dough quite thinly on a lightly floured surface and cut out the biscuits using a heart-shaped cutter. Lightly knead any trimmings together and re-roll.

4 Place the biscuits on a lightly greased baking sheet and bake in a preheated oven, 190°C/375°F/Gas Mark 5, for 25-30 minutes, until golden brown.

5 Sprinkle the caster or icing sugar over the biscuits while they are still hot.

Preparation time: about 15 minutes
Cooking time: 25-30 minutes
Oven temperature: 190°C/375°F/Gas Mark 5

Little Chocolate Boxes

- **250 g/8 oz plain dark chocolate**
- **3 eggs**
- **75 g/3 oz caster sugar**
- **grated rind of 1 orange**
- **75 g/3 oz plain flour**
- **pinch of salt**
- **2 tablespoons Curaçao**
- **4 tablespoons apricot jam, warmed and sieved**
- **150 ml/¼ pint double cream, whipped**
- **6 strawberries, halved**

1 Melt the chocolate in a bowl set over a pan of hot water. Pour it on to a piece of waxed paper to make a 30 x 23 cm/ 12 x 9 inch rectangle and leave to cool.

2 Whisk the eggs, sugar and orange rind in a bowl set over a pan of simmering water, until they are thick and light.

3 Sift in the flour and salt, and fold in gently.

Turn the mixture into a greased and lined 28 x 18 x 4 cm/11 x 7 x 1½ inch Swiss roll tin and bake in a preheated oven, 220°C/425°F/Gas Mark 7, for 10 minutes until light golden in colour and springy to the touch. Turn out to cool on a wire tray.

4 Sprinkle the cake with the orange Curaçao and cut it into 12 equal cubes about 5 x 6 cm/2 x 2½ inches.

5 Brush the sides of each square with a little warmed and sieved apricot jam.

6 Cut the chocolate into 48 squares to fit the sides of the cakes, and press them on to the sides.

7 Spoon or pipe whipped cream into the boxes and top each with half a strawberry.

Makes 12
Preparation time: 30 minutes
Cooking time: 10 minutes
Oven temperature: 220°C/425°F/Gas Mark 7

Chocolate Pear Heart Cake

- **1 large pear, peeled and sliced**
- **50 g/2 oz self-raising flour**
- **50 g/2 oz butter**
- **1 egg**
- **50 g/2 oz caster sugar**
- **1 tablespoon cocoa powder**
- **½ teaspoon instant coffee granules dissolved in 1 teaspoon hot water**
- **¼ teaspoon baking powder**
- **1 teaspoon Calvados, to serve**

1 Line a small heart-shaped baking tin with greaseproof paper. Arrange the pear slices on the greaseproof paper in the baking tin.

2 Using an electric mixer or food processor, mix the flour, butter, egg, sugar, cocoa, liquid coffee and baking powder until smooth.
3 Spread this mixture over the pears and level the surface.
4 Bake in a moderately hot oven, 190°C/375°F/Gas Mark 5, for 30–35 minutes until it has the appearance of a fully baked cake.
5 Unmould the cake and leave it to cool on a wire rack with the pears uppermost. Serve cold, sprinkled with the Calvados and accompanied by cream or ice-cream.

Preparation time: 20 minutes, plus cooling
Cooking time: 30–35 minutes
Oven temperature: 190°C/375°F/Gas Mark 5

Chocolate Valentine Cake

- **4 eggs**
- **125 g/4 oz caster sugar**
- **125 g/4 oz plain flour**
- **25 g/1 oz butter, melted**
- **25 g/1 oz hazelnuts, finely ground**
- **300 ml/½ pint whipping cream**
- **50 g/2 oz plain chocolate, grated**
- **250 g/8 oz firm strawberries**
- **icing sugar, for dusting (optional)**

CHOCOLATE GANACHE:
- **300 g/10 oz plain chocolate, broken into pieces**
- **150 ml/¼ pint double or whipping cream**

1 Grease and flour two 18 cm/7 inch heart-shaped tins, measured at the widest part.

2 Beat together the eggs and sugar in a bowl, then place the bowl over a saucepan of very hot, but not boiling, water. Beat until the mixture becomes thick and creamy and leaves a trail when a little of the mixture is pulled across the surface. Remove from the heat and continue to beat until the mixture is cold. (If using an electric beater, added heat is not necessary.)

3 Sift half the flour over the surface of the mixture. Add half the melted butter. With a metal spoon, fold in the flour using a cutting figure-of-eight action until all the flour has been incorporated. Repeat with the remaining flour, the hazelnuts and the remaining butter. Fold as lightly and as little as possible.

4 Pour the mixture into the prepared tins and tilt until the mixture spreads evenly over the tins.

5 Place in a preheated oven, 180°C/350°F/Gas Mark 4, for 15–20 minutes until the sponge is well risen and golden brown, and springs back when lightly pressed with a finger. Turn out on to a wire rack to cool.

6 When the cakes are cool, split each heart into two layers. Whip the cream, fold in the grated chocolate and spread one-third of the cream on one heart.

7 Reserve 3 strawberries with stalks for decoration. Spread the ganache on the top and sides of the cakes and decorate with the strawberries. Chop the remaining strawberries roughly.

8 Spread the chopped strawberries over the first layer of cream, smooth over a little more cream and sandwich with a second layer of sponge. Divide the remaining cream in 2 and sandwich the remaining sponges with the cream, ending with a layer of sponge. Stand the cake on a wire rack with a large plate underneath.

9 To make the chocolate ganache, place the chocolate in a heatproof bowl set over a pan of hot water. When the chocolate has melted, stir until smooth. Meanwhile, pour the cream into a separate pan and bring just to the boil. Gradually pour the cream into the melted chocolate, stirring vigorously until the mixture is smooth.

10 Pour the hot chocolate ganache over the cake and smooth it over quickly with a small palette knife. Leave to set for about 15 minutes.

11 Arrange the sliced strawberries in a row around the base of the cake. Place the three whole strawberries in a cluster on top.

12 Leave the cake to set for about 2 hours. If liked, give it a very light sprinkling of icing sugar just before serving.

Makes an 18 cm/7 inch cake
Preparation time: 1 hour, plus cooling
Cooking time: 15–20 minutes
Oven temperature: 180°C/350°F/Gas Mark 4

Chocolate Truffles

- **3 tablespoons double cream**
- **325 g/9 oz plain chocolate, broken into small pieces**
- **½-1 tablespoon whisky or cognac (optional)**
- **2 tablespoons cocoa powder, for dusting**

1 Heat the cream gently until tepid. Put 125 g/4 oz of the chocolate pieces into a small basin and melt gently over hot, but not boiling, water, stirring occasionally. Do not rest the basin in the hot water. Remove the bowl from the heat and slowly pour in the cream stirring thoroughly.

2 Cool the mixture and add whisky or cognac. Whisk for 3–4 minutes until the mixture becomes lighter and stands in peaks. Cool in the refrigerator for about 20 minutes.

3 Sieve the cocoa powder on to a tray or board. Roll spoonfuls of the chocolate paste into balls about 2.5 cm/1 inch in diameter. Roll each into the cocoa powder to cover. Leave to cool until firm.

4 To cover the truffle balls in chocolate, melt the remaining 200 g/7 oz of plain chocolate over hot water. Spear each truffle on a skewer and dip them one by one into the melted chocolate. Place them on a marble slab or tin foil to set.

Makes 10 truffles
Preparation time: 40 minutes, plus chilling

Viennese Chocolate Whirls

- **250 g/8 oz butter or block margarine, softened, plus extra for greasing**
- **50 g/2 oz icing sugar**
- **½ teaspoon vanilla essence**
- **250 g/8 oz plain flour**
- **25 g/1 oz drinking chocolate powder**
- **50 g/2 oz cornflour**

TO DECORATE:
- **125 g/4 oz dipping or cooking chocolate**
- **icing sugar, to dust**

1 Cream together the butter and icing sugar until light and fluffy. Add the vanilla essence and beat well. Sift the flour, chocolate powder and cornflour over the mixture and whisk until smooth.

2 Fill a large piping bag fitted with a 2 cm/¾ inch star nozzle and pipe 'S' shapes on to 2 greased baking sheets. Bake in a preheated oven, 180°C/350°F/Gas Mark 4, for about 25 minutes, then lift on to a wire tray to cool.

3 Melt the chocolate in a small heatproof bowl set over a saucepan of hot water. Stir until smooth. Dip half of each biscuit into the chocolate and cool until set on greaseproof paper.

4 Line up the biscuits with the chocolate ends in one direction. Cover the chocolate loosely with greaseproof paper and dust the uncovered ends with icing sugar.

Makes about 20
Preparation time: 20 minutes, plus cooling and setting
Cooking time: about 25 minutes
Oven temperature: 180°C/350°F/Gas Mark 4

Passion Cake

- 175 g/6 oz young carrots
- 75 g/3 oz shelled walnuts
- 175 g/6 oz butter or margarine
- 175 g/6 oz soft brown sugar
- 3 large eggs
- 175 g/6 oz wholemeal self-raising flour, sifted with 1½ teaspoons baking powder
- 50 g/2 oz ground almonds
- 1 tablespoon milk

TO DECORATE:
- 350 g/12 oz Quark or curd cheese
- halved or chopped walnuts
- icing sugar, sieved (optional)

1 Grease and flour or line a 20 cm/8 inch cake tin. Preheat the oven to 180°C/350°F, Gas Mark 4.

2 Peel and finely grate the carrots just before making the cake. Do not soak them in water. Coarsely chop the walnuts.

3 Cream the butter or margarine and sugar until soft and light.

4 Beat the eggs and gradually blend into the creamed mixture.

5 Fold in the flour and baking powder with the ground almonds. Add the carrot, chopped walnuts and milk. Mix thoroughly, then spoon into the prepared tin. Bake in the preheated oven for 1 hour, or until firm to the touch. Cool for 5 minutes in the tin.

6 Split the cold cake through the centre and spread with a layer of Quark or curd cheese. Top with another layer of Quark or curd cheese, and decorate with halved or chopped walnuts or with icing sugar, if liked.

Makes a 20 cm/8 inch cake
Preparation time: 30 minutes
Cooking time: 1 hour
Oven temperature: 180°C/350°F/Gas Mark 4

Better is a dinner of herbs where love is,
than a stalled ox and hatred therewith.

PROVERBS 15:17

Celebration Menus

FIRST IMPRESSIONS

The food may be impressive but none of the courses is difficult to prepare. Make sure that the soup is really smooth, that the duck is not overcooked, and that the chocolate mousse is really well chilled.

**ARTICHOKE AND HAZELNUT SOUP
DUCK WITH BLACKCURRANT SAUCE
FRENCH BEAN BUNDLES
CHOCOLATE MOUSSE**

Artichoke and Hazelnut Soup

- 75 g/3 oz shelled hazelnuts, lightly toasted
- 1 x 400 g/14 oz can artichoke hearts
- 1 small onion, chopped
- 450 ml/¾ pint chicken stock
- 15 g/½ oz butter
- 1 tablespoon plain flour
- 150 ml/¼ pint single cream
- salt and freshly ground black pepper

TO GARNISH:
- 1 tablespoon hazelnuts, lightly toasted and chopped
- watercress sprigs

1 Put the hazelnuts in a blender or food processor and crush them coarsely. Transfer to a saucepan.
2 Drain the liquid from the artichoke hearts and add to the pan. Roughly chop 3 of the artichoke hearts and add with the onion and chicken stock. Bring to the boil and simmer for 20 minutes.
3 Allow to cool thoroughly, then strain in the flavoured stock.
4 Melt the butter in a saucepan. Stir in the flour and cook for 1 minute. Gradually stir in the flavoured stock. Finely chop the remaining artichoke hearts and add. Simmer gently for about 5–10 minutes.
5 Purée the soup in the blender or food processor until smooth. Pour the soup into a clean saucepan. Stir in the cream and heat through gently. Add salt and pepper to taste. Serve in soup bowls, garnished with the chopped hazelnuts and watercress.

Preparation time: 15 minutes, plus cooling
Cooking time: 45 minutes

French Bean Bundles

- 175 g/6 oz French beans, topped and tailed
- 25 g/1 oz butter
- 1 canned red pimento, cut into 4 long thin strips
- salt and freshly ground black pepper

1 Cook the beans in sufficient boiling salted water to half-cover the beans, until just tender. Drain the beans thoroughly and return to the pan.
2 Add the butter, salt and pepper to taste and toss well.
3 Divide the beans into 4 bundles, and lay a strip of pimento over each one, overlapping the ends. Serve hot.

Preparation time: 10 minutes
Cooking time: 6–8 minutes

Duck with Blackcurrant Sauce

- 1 oven-ready duck 1.5 kg/3½ lb, halved
- 1 tablespoon chopped fresh rosemary
- 4 tablespoons brandy
- olive oil
- salt and freshly ground black pepper
- fresh rosemary, to garnish
SAUCE:
- 25 g/1 oz butter
- 1 small onion, finely chopped
- 1 x 300 g/10 oz blackcurrants in syrup
- 2 tablespoons red wine vinegar

1 Put the halved duck into a large shallow dish. Pierce in a few places with a fine skewer. Add salt and pepper to taste, the chopped rosemary, brandy and a sprinkling of olive oil. Cover and marinate in the refrigerator for at least 6 hours or overnight.
2 Remove the duck, reserving any marinade. Place the duck halves on a rack in a roasting tin, skin side uppermost. Rub a little olive oil into the duck skin. Roast in a preheated oven, 200°C/400°F/Gas Mark 6, for 1 hour or until the duck is tender.
3 Meanwhile, prepare the sauce. Melt the butter in a saucepan, add the onion and fry gently for 3 minutes. Add the blackcurrants in their syrup, wine vinegar and reserved duck marinade. Bring to the boil and simmer gently for 5 minutes.
4 Purée the sauce in a blender or food processor until smooth. Return to the saucepan and heat through. Taste and adjust the seasoning if necessary.
5 Place the duck halves on a serving dish, spoon the sauce over the top and garnish with rosemary. Serve accompanied by French bean bundles.

Preparation time: 20 minutes, plus marinating
Cooking time: 1 hour 10 minutes
Oven temperature: 200°C/400°F/Gas Mark 6

Chocolate Mousse

- 75 g/3 oz bitter dark chocolate, broken into pieces
- 25 g/1 oz plain chocolate, broken into pieces
- 25 g/1 oz butter
- 2 eggs, separated
- 1 tablespoon ginger wine
- 150 ml/¼ pint double cream
- 50 g/2 oz caster sugar
- little chopped crystallized ginger, to decorate

1 Place the chocolate in a heatproof bowl with the butter. Stand over a pan of hot water and stir until the chocolate has melted. Allow to cool slightly.
2 Whisk the egg yolks with the ginger wine until creamy. Whip the cream until thick.
3 Stir the whisked egg yolk mixture into the melted chocolate, then fold in the whipped cream. Whisk the egg whites until thick and foamy. Add half the sugar and whisk until stiff. Finally, whisk in the remaining sugar. Fold into the chocolate mixture lightly but thoroughly. Spoon into stemmed sundae dishes and chill.
4 Serve decorated with a little chopped crystallized ginger.

Preparation time: 20–25 minutes, plus chilling

A MEAL TO WARM THE HEART

This is the perfect food to serve in cold weather. Although the starter and dessert are both served cold to help with the preparation, one is served with fingers of hot toast and the other is topped with a hot rum sauce.

CHOPPED LIVER PATE
CHICORY AND BEETROOT SALAD
PORK NOISETTES WITH RICH ONION SAUCE
RATAFIA ICE-CREAM WITH HOT RUM SAUCE

Chopped Liver Pâté

- 50 g/2 oz butter
- 1 small onion, finely chopped
- 175 g/6 oz chicken livers, trimmed and chopped
- 1 garlic clove, crushed
- 2 hard-boiled eggs
- salt and freshly ground black pepper

1 Heat the butter in a frying pan. Add the onion and fry gently until soft. Add the chicken livers, garlic and salt and pepper to taste and cook until the livers are sealed on the outside but still pink in the centre.

2 Tip the liver mixture ino a bowl and finely chop, using 2 sharp knives in a criss-cross motion.

3 Separate the hard-boiled egg whites from the yolks. Chop the egg white finely and stir into the liver. Push the egg yolks through a sieve and reserve. (For a smoother texture, the liver mixture and egg white can be puréed in a blender or food processor.)

4 Chill the pâté for 1–2 hours. Garnish with the sieved egg yolks and serve with triangles of hot toast.

Preparation time: 10–15 minutes, plus chilling
Cooking time: 4–5 minutes

Chicory and Beetroot Salad

- 1 large beetroot, cooked, peeled and thinly sliced
- 1 small head of chicory, finely shredded
- grated rind and juice of ½ orange
- 4 tablespoons olive oil
- salt and freshly grated black pepper

1 Arrange the beetroot slices in a shallow serving dish. Sprinkle over the chicory.

2 Mix the orange rind and juice with the olive oil, and add salt and pepper to taste. Spoon the dressing evenly over the salad. Do not leave the salad standing for too long before serving, or the colour will leak from the beetroot into the chicory.

Preparation time: 15 minutes

Pork Noisettes with Rich Onion Sauce

- **2 lean pork chops, boned**
- **25 g/1 oz butter**
- **1 large onion, finely sliced**
- **2 tablespoons red wine vinegar**
- **1 tablespoon dark brown sugar**
- **5 tablespoons water or stock**
- **2 tablespoons medium sherry**
- **salt and freshly ground black pepper**

1 Curl each pork chop round in the shape of a noisette and tie securely with fine string.
2 Heat the butter in a frying pan. Add the onion and fry gently for 3 minutes. Add the pork noisettes, fry gently for 6–8 minutes and keep warm.
3 Add the wine vinegar, brown sugar, water or stock, sherry and salt and pepper to taste to the pan. Bring to the boil and simmer gently for 4 minutes, stirring frequently.
4 Add the noisettes and heat through gently. Serve hot with mashed potatoes.

Preparation time: 20 minutes
Cooking time: 25 minutes

Ratafia Ice-cream with Hot Rum Sauce

- **150 ml/¼ pint double cream**
- **2 teaspoons instant coffee powder**
- **1 tablespoon hot water**
- **150 ml/¼ pint custard, pouring consistency**
- **2 tablespoons crushed ratafia biscuits or macaroons**
SAUCE:
- **3 tablespoons apricot jam**
- **2 tablespoons rum**
- **1 tablespoon raisins**

1 Whip the cream until thick. Dissolve the coffee powder in the hot water. Fold into the whipped cream with the custard. Put into a freezer tray and freeze until the mixture starts to harden at the edges.
2 Tip into a bowl and beat until slushy. Stir in the ratafias. Return the mixture to the tray, then to the freezer and freeze until firm.
3 To make the sauce, sieve the apricot jam into a saucepan. Add the rum and raisins and heat through gently, stirring frequently.
4 Scoop the ice-cream into serving dishes and spoon the hot sauce over the top. Serve immediately.

Preparation time: 15–20 minutes, plus freezing
Cooking time: 2–3 minutes

FEAST TO CELEBRATE

Marinated raw smoked salmon, plump steaks with a tangy soured cream sauce, and a deliciously refreshing melon tart are the elegant components of this menu which help to mark a special occasion.

**CEVICHE OF SALMON
STUFFED TOMATOES
FILLET STEAK PIQUANT
CHOCOLATE MOUSSE TARTLETS**

Ceviche of Salmon

• 1 x 175 g/6 oz piece of salmon fillet
• lemon juice, for sprinkling
• olive oil, for sprinkling
• salt and freshly ground black pepper
• fresh dill or fennel sprigs, to garnish

1 Using a sharp knife, cut down through the fillet of salmon into very thin slices – about the same thickness as sliced smoked salmon. Arrange the raw salmon on two plates in a single layer.
2 Sprinkle the salmon with lemon juice and olive oil, and season to taste with salt and pepper.
3 Garnish with snipped fresh dill or fennel. Serve immediately with brown bread and butter.

Preparation time: 20 minutes

Stuffed Tomatoes

• 4 medium tomatoes
• 125 g/4 oz frozen peas
• 25 g/1 oz butter
• generous pinch of ground mace
• 1 tablespoon double cream
• salt and freshly ground black pepper
• small parsley sprigs, to garnish

1 Cut a thin slice from the non-stalk end of each tomato and carefully hollow out the centre. (Reserve the centres for use in soups, sauces, etc.) Carefully dry the inside of each tomato with kitchen paper.
2 Arrange the tomatoes in an ovenproof dish. Place in a preheated oven 160°C/325°F/Gas Mark 3, and heat through for 5 minutes.
3 Meanwhile, put the peas into a saucepan with the butter, mace, cream and salt and pepper to taste. Cover and simmer gently until the peas are tender. Mash the peas to a smooth paste and beat in the cream.
4 Fill the hollowed-out tomatoes with the creamy pea purée, cover with foil and return to the oven. Heat for a further 3–4 minutes. Serve hot, garnished with parsley.

Preparation time: 15 minutes
Cooking time: about 18 minutes
Oven temperature: 160°C/325°F/Gas Mark 3

Fillet Steak Piquant

- 2 fillet steaks, cut about 2.5 cm/1 inch thick
- 25 g/1 oz butter
- 1 small garlic clove, crushed
- 1 teaspoon Worcestershire sauce
- 1 teaspoon grated fresh horseradish
- 75 ml/3 fl oz soured cream
- salt and freshly ground black pepper
- ½ small red pepper, cored, deseeded and finely chopped, to garnish

1 Season the steaks with salt and pepper. Heat the butter in a large frying pan. Add the garlic and the steaks and fry gently for 3 minutes on each side. Remove the steaks and keep warm. (If you like your meat cooked well done, cook the steaks for slightly longer.)

2 Add the Worcestershire sauce to the cooking juices in the pan and bring to the boil. Remove the pan from the heat and whisk in the horseradish and soured cream.

3 Return the steaks to the sauce in the pan and heat through gently without boiling. Garnish with the red pepper, and serve with stuffed tomatoes and sautéed new potatoes.

Preparation time: 3 minutes
Cooking time: 10 minutes

Chocolate Mousse Tartlets

- 125 g/4 oz plain flour
- 50 g/2 oz chilled butter, diced
- 25 g/1 oz caster sugar
- 1 small egg, beaten
- icing sugar, for dusting

FILLING:
- 75 g/3 oz dark chocolate, broken into squares
- 1 tablespoon water
- 5 g/¼ oz unsalted butter
- 1 teaspoon brandy or Cointreau
- 2 small eggs, separated

1 Place the flour in a bowl, add the butter and rub in with the fingertips until the mixture resembles fine breadcrumbs. Stir in the sugar, then add the egg and mix to a firm dough, adding a little water if necessary.

2 Turn the dough out on a lightly floured surface and knead briefly. Roll out and line a 4 x 7.5 cm/3 inch deep tartlet tin. Reroll the trimmings and line a 2 more tins. Fill each with crumpled foil and place on a baking sheet. Bake in a preheated oven, 200°C/400°F/Gas Mark 6, for 15 minutes, remove the foil and return the tartlets to the oven for another 5 minutes. Leave to cool.

3 Make the filling. Place the chocolate in a heatproof bowl. Add the water. Set the bowl over a pan of hot water and leave until the chocolate has melted, stirring occasionally.

4 Remove the bowl from over the water and stir in the butter until it has melted. Add the brandy or Cointreau. Stir in the egg yolks. Whisk the egg whites in a grease-free bowl until they are stiff and dry. Fold into the chocolate mixture.

5 Spoon the mousse mixture into the pastry cases, then transfer to the refrigerator for 2–3 hours, until set. Dust the tartlets lightly with sifted icing sugar before serving. Serve cold.

Makes 6
Preparation time: 25 minutes, plus chilling
Cooking time: 20 minutes
Oven temperature: 200°C/400°F/Gas Mark 6

Aïoli, lobster and asparagus salad with 44
almonds: strawberry meringue heart 56
apples: apple sorbet 66
roast pheasant flambéed with Calvados 33
apricots, pork with orange and 26
artichokes: artichoke and hazelnut soup 84
eggs with creamed spinach and hollandaise sauce 19
asparagus: lobster and asparagus salad with aïoli 44
lobster and asparagus salad with herb dressing 44
avocados: avocado and grapefruit salad 48-9
Parma ham with avocado 20

Banana and coconut tart 52
beef: fillet steak piquant 95
fillet steak with smoked oysters 26
Indonesian steak with chilli 30
tournedos en croûte 28-9
beetroot and chicory salad 88
biscuits: heart biscuits 73
lipstick biscuits 72
Viennese chocolate whirls 79
blackcurrants: brown bread and blackcurrant ice cream 59
duck with blackcurrant sauce 87
bread: brown bread and blackcurrant ice cream 59
brown bread and chocolate chip ice cream 59
chocolate and cinnamon bread and butter pudding 60-1

Cakes: chocolate pear heart cake 74-5
chocolate Valentine cake 76
little chocolate boxes 74
passion cake 80
sweetheart cake 70
Calvados, roast pheasant flambéed with 33
carrots: carrots with ginger and almonds 46
heart biscuits 73
passion cake 80

celery and melon salad 48
ceviche of salmon 92
champagne sorbet 65
cheese, soft: chocolate hearts 62
passion cake 80
red fruit salad with coeurs à la crème 56
chestnut roulade 55
chicken livers: chopped liver pâté 88
chicory and beetroot salad 88
chillies: Indonesian steak with chilli 30
spicy butterflied prawns 18
chocolate 8-9
brown bread and chocolate chip ice cream 59
chocolate and cinnamon bread and butter pudding 60-1
chocolate fruity fondue 62
chocolate hearts 62
chocolate mousse 87
chocolate mousse tartlets 95
chocolate pear heart cake 74-5
chocolate truffles 79
chocolate Valentine cake 76
decorations 8-9
hot chocolate liqueur soufflé 60
little chocolate boxes 74
melting 8
Viennese chocolate whirls 79
cocoa powder 8
coconut and banana tart 52
coeurs à la crème, red fruit salad with 56
crab salad, spicy 42
cranberry sorbet 65
Crème de Menthe: hot chocolate liqueur soufflé 60
curls, chocolate 9

Decorations, chocolate 8-9
desserts 50-66
duck with blackcurrant sauce 87

Eggs: eggs with creamed spinach and hollandaise sauce 19
Florence-style eggs 15
quails' egg tartlets 12
exotic fruit salad 52

Figs: venison with port and fresh figs 29

fillet steak piquant 95
fillet steak with smoked oysters 26
fish see haddock; salmon; smoked salmon
Florence-style eggs 15
flowers 7-8
fondue, chocolate fruity 62
French bean bundles 84
fruit: chocolate fruity fondue 62
exotic fruit salad 52
red fruit salad with coeurs à la crème 56

Garlic: lobster and asparagus salad with aïoli 44
grapefruit and avocado salad 48-9
grapes, potato salad with smoked salmon, pecan nuts and 12
Green Goddess dressing, lobster with 34

Haddock: lemon-fried fish with mushrooms and mangetout 38
ham: Parma ham with avocado 20
timbales of Parma ham 22
Hawaiian salad 49
hazelnuts: artichoke and hazelnut soup 84
heart biscuits 73
hollandaise sauce, eggs with creamed spinach and 19
horseradish: fillet steak piquant 95

Ice cream: brown bread and blackcurrant 59
brown bread and chocolate chip 59
ratafia ice cream with hot rum sauce 91
Indonesian steak with chilli 30

Lamb: noisettes of lamb with pomegranates 32
leaves, chocolate 9
lemon-fried fish with mushrooms and mangetout 38
lipstick biscuits 72
little chocolate boxes 74
liver: chopped liver pâté 88
warm salad with calves' liver 16
lobster: lobster and asparagus salad with aïoli 44

lobster and asparagus salad with herb dressing 44
lobster thermidor 34
lobster with Green Goddess dressing 34

Mangetout, lemon-fried fish with mushrooms and 38
mayonnaise 42
lobster and asparagus salad with aïoli 44
melon and celery salad 48
melting chocolate 8
meringue heart, strawberry 56
microwave ovens, melting chocolate in 8
milk chocolate 8
mousses: chocolate mousse 87
chocolate mousse tartlets 95
mushrooms: lemon-fried fish with mushrooms and mangetout 38
oyster mushroom salad 46
wild mushroom feuilleté 15

Onions: pork noisettes with rich onion sauce 91
orange, pork with apricots and 26
oyster mushroom salad 46
oysters: fillet steak with smoked oysters 26
oysters in cream sauce 20
smoked oyster tarts 16

Parma ham: Parma ham with avocado 20
timbales of Parma ham 22
passion cake 80
passionfruit sorbet 64
pâté, chopped liver 88
pears: chocolate pear heart cake 74-5
pear sorbet 66
peas: stuffed tomatoes 92
pecan nuts, potato salad with smoked salmon, grapes and 12
pheasant: roast pheasant flambéed with Calvados 33
plain chocolate 8
pomegranates, noisettes of lamb with 32
pork: pork noisettes with rich onion sauce 91
pork with orange and apricots 26

potato salad with smoked salmon, grapes and pecan nuts 12
prawns: oysters in cream sauce 20
potato salad with smoked salmon, grapes and pecan nuts 12
spicy butterflied prawns 18

Quails' egg tartlets 12

Ratafia ice cream with hot rum sauce 91
red fruit salad with coeurs à la crème 56
roulade, chestnut 55
rum: ratafia ice cream with hot rum sauce 91

Salads 42-9
avocado and grapefruit salad 48-9
chicory and beetroot salad 88
Hawaiian salad 49
lobster and asparagus salad with aïoli 44
lobster and asparagus salad with herb dressing 44
melon and celery salad 48
oyster mushroom salad 46
potato salad with smoked salmon, grapes and pecan nuts 12
spicy crab salad 42
warm salad with calves' liver 16
salmon: ceviche of salmon 92
pan-fried salmon with crème fraîche and fresh watercress 36
pan-fried salmon with tomato coulis 36
see also smoked salmon
shortbread: strawberry shortbread creams 55
smoked oyster tarts 16
smoked salmon: Hawaiian salad 49
potato salad with smoked salmon, grapes and pecan nuts 12
timbales of smoked salmon 22
sorbets: apple 66
champagne 65
cranberry 65
passionfruit 64
pear 66
soufflé, hot chocolate liqueur 60
soup, artichoke and

hazelnut 84
spicy butterflied prawns 18
spicy crab salad 42
spinach: eggs with creamed spinach and hollandaise sauce 19
Florence-style eggs 15
starters 11-22
strawberries: chocolate Valentine cake 76
strawberry meringue heart 56
strawberry shortbread creams 55
sweetheart cake 70

Tarts: banana and coconut tart 52
chocolate mousse tartlets 95
quails' egg tartlets 12
smoked oyster tarts 16
timbales of Parma ham 22
timbales of smoked salmon 22
tomatoes: pan-fried salmon with tomato coulis 36
stuffed tomatoes 92
tournedos en croûte 28-9
truffles, chocolate 79

Valentine cake, chocolate 76
venison with port and fresh figs 29
Viennese chocolate whirls 79

Walnuts: passion cake 80
watercress: pan-fried salmon with crème fraîche and fresh watercress 36
white chocolate 8

Special Photography:
Simon Smith
Home Economists:
Lucy Knox, Sarah Lowman
Recipe Photography:
Reed Consumer Books Ltd./
Theo Bergstrom, Martin Brigdale, Nick Carman, Laurie Evans, Amanda Heywood, Jeremy Hopley, Sue Jorgensen, David Jorgensen, David Jordan, Fred Mancini, James Murphy, Peter Myers, Alan Newham, Charlie Stebbings, Clive Streeter
Jacket Photography:
Philip Webb and Simon Smith
Jacket Home Economists:
Fran Warde, Lucy Knox and Sarah Lowman